A CONCISE GUIDE TO
DREAMS

A CONCISE GUIDE TO
DREAMS

Philip Clucas & Douglas Clucas

Bath · New York · Singapore · Hong Kong · Cologne · Delhi · Melbourne

This edition published in 2008
Parragon
Queen Street House
4 Queen Street
Bath BA1 1HE, UK

CONCEIVED AND PRODUCED BY Focus
Publishing, Sevenoaks, Kent

PROJECT EDITOR Guy Croton

DESIGNER Philip Clucas MCSD

INDEXER Caroline Watson

A catalogue record of this book is available from the British Library.

ISBN 978-1-4075-1138-2

Printed in China

CONTENTS

THE WORLD OF DREAMS

We sleep to revive our bodies and minds. It is through this process that we are able to prepare ourselves for the stresses and strains that await us in everyday life, as well as for the physical challenges we put our bodies through each day.

Generally our sleep patterns follow a regular rhythm of approximately 90 minutes, and each night progress through four distinct phases of increasingly deeper sleep. This process begins with light sleep when our bodies first relax, and culminates in the fourth period of deep sleep which usually lasts between 30 and 40 minutes.

It is during the periods of milder sleep that dreaming is likely to occur – when our minds are fairly active. We retain sensory function, and dream visions are more easily received and influenced by the subconscious mind.

With hindsight our dreams may seem strange and alien to our conscious being, but they represent the 'spin' our psyche puts upon our emotional desires and fears, rather than a direct portrayal of our waking lives. This book will help you to explore your dreams, and gain an understanding of the hidden messages they impart.

DREAM CATEGORIES

I t is generally accepted that dreams can be divided into nine separate categories; understanding which of these groups our dreams fall into is the first stage towards interpreting them.

Psychological Healing Dreams

Although these dreams can be frightening or disturbing at times, they are different from nightmares because they represent real situations we may find ourselves in during our daily lives. Often these dreams occur at times of stress or when we have important and extremely hard decisions to make. These dreams should not be viewed negatively, as they often help us heal ourselves, free us from negative emotions and clear the way for future growth and change.

Problem Solving Dreams

These dreams usually include a 'guide' or 'helper' who imparts to the sleeper an important message which may help them to solve a problem in their waking lives. It is important to note that it is not just the image shown to the dreamer that is relevant to understanding the dream, but the person revealing this information to the sleeper is also paramount.

Physiological Dreams

Some dreams are merely a direct representation of our emotional, psychological or physical desires. To dream that you are thirsty may simply express the fact that your body craves extra fluid, or to dream that you are walking over a frozen lake might reflect your need for

Right: *Spiritual guides may take the form of a friend, stranger or even an animal messenger. If the dreamer finds themselves lost at sea they may be guided to shore by a dolphin. Occasionally animals may speak to the sleeper and offer pertinent advice.*

Right: Images of childhood are common in our dreams because they represent a carefree time when we were protected and loved unconditionally. Such psychological dreams represent a desire for comfort or stability.

an extra blanket to warm the bed. This can be carried into our emotions, where the conscious and subconscious become intermixed and entangled.

Dreams of Daily Life

Dreams of familiar faces, places and events can feel important – precisely because they seem so real. However, they are often among the least instructive of dreams because they are simple echoes of the waking world reflected in our slumbers. Such dreams can be inspired by real disturbances; for example the muffled sound of traffic outside a window can instigate dreams of driving.

Premonition/Clairvoyant Dreams

Most people will have experienced premonitions in their dreams that appear later to have come true. However, rather than displaying any clairvoyant skills, such dreams are common and have a more rational explanation. During our waking lives our brain absorbs a huge amount of information, both consciously and subconsciously; this includes various prompts about the likely behaviour of others, especially those we are close to. When people or events unfold as we have 'foreseen' we believe them to be prophetic, but in fact they are merely the logical unfolding of events that our subconscious deduces.

Recurring Dreams

Dreams that repeat themselves are a sign of troubles that remain unsolved in our waking lives. Our psyche uses sleep to remind us of the anxieties we feel, the problems we have to resolve and the stresses and strains we are under. These feelings can be expressed in a myriad different ways, though occasionally when the mind discovers a particularly effective method of highlighting these tensions it will repeat it until the dreamer resolves the issues that are troubling them.

Lucid Dreams

In these dreams the sleeper often knows that they are dreaming. The dream will feel real, but events or characters will be greatly exaggerated. The sleeper will often manipulate these dreams to their own advantage – and thus is offered up a positive tool to explore new vistas and help resolve conflict.

Compensatory Dreams

Some of our dreams allow us to do things we would never contemplate in waking life, while others reveal 'shadowed' sides to our personality. Shy people may experience flamboyant images of themselves, whilst those who are usually sexually restrained might dream that they are ravenously promiscuous. Such dreams are designed to balance our personality and give vent to emotions we would not usually seek to experience.

Nightmares

Nightmares are the most emotionally draining of all dreams and will be discussed in greater detail later in the book. They represent concerns in our waking lives which our subconscious mind seeks to emphasize by fearfully impelling our attention. Although our dreams can never physically harm us – and even seemingly terrifying dreams are sent to help us – persistent nightmares can be draining if they regularly occur, so it is advisable to confide them to a friend or even a professional counsellor.

Right: Nightmares were once thought to be the work of demons – more specifically incubi – which were thought to sit on the chests of sleepers. In his painting 'The Nightmare' Henry Fuseli conveys the terror that such dreams engender. However, by understanding and eventual confrontation, such visions can invariably be banished (see pages 244–7).

DREAM BELIEFS

Long before written records began, dreams were considered significant. They have played a part in shaping all major world religions. From Jacob's dreams of angels ascending to heaven, to Mohammed's visionary inspiration for his spiritual mission, dreamlore has been vital to shaping the course, not just of our religious beliefs, but also of world history. Because of their importance, mankind has always been fascinated by trying to understand and analyze dreams, and every culture has its own beliefs and customs surrounding the dreamscape.

The ancient Babylonians divided dreams into the good (inspired by benign spirits) and the bad (aroused by demons); though it was the Assyrians who first connected dreams to divine prophecy. They thought that in sleep one could transcend the boundaries of mortal life and enter the spiritual realm, where one would be blessed with a prophetic message.

To the Egyptians, dreamlore was even more important. Priests believed that the gods revealed their intentions only through dreams – and never during our waking lives. Because of this they built designated

Left and above right: *Anubis was the Egyptian god of the dead – often depicted holding a pair of scales: these represent the balance of the individual's soul. In Ancient Egypt it was believed that to receive a vision in a dream (the gift of the gods) your body and soul had to be in equilibrium.*

shrines where those blessed with a particular ability to bridge the temporal realm could go to sleep and await divine enlightenment. These temples were decorated with statues of the gods – especially Anubus – to help inspire the sleepers.

To the Jews the will of Jehovah was regularly revealed in dreams and the Old Testament is scattered with dream-inspired revelations. Perhaps the best known is Pharaoh's dream of 'seven fat cows' eaten by 'seven thin cows' and 'seven healthy ears of corn' followed by 'seven diseased ears of corn', which Joseph interpreted to foretell the seven years of plenty followed by seven years of famine that affected Egypt. Prophets such as Elijah, Samuel and Solomon also received divine messages through dreams which, like Joseph and Daniel, elevated their position at court.

One of the most important dreams to the Jewish religion is that of Jacob. He dreamed that he saw angels climbing a ladder to heaven *(below)* and heard God

promise that he and his family would own the land where they slept. Years later he changed his name to 'Israel' and even today the descendants of the Twelve Tribes that he sired still lay claim to the land.

The final chapter of the New Testament is also dedicated to a dream. Through it Saint Paul foretells of the destruction of the world, and it is perhaps the most controversial and least understood of all chapters of the Bible. Throughout the Middle Ages the coming of the Apocalypse (eagerly awaited by some) shaped doctrine and inspired avoidable atrocities.

Islam was founded upon the revelations given to Mohammed in his sleep and, as in Judaism, dreamlore is considered important. Hindus respect the guidance of 'sleeping wisdom', while in Japan shrines for 'incubating dreams' still exist today.

The ancient Celts believed that revelations in dreams foretell when best to hunt, or even to go to war. Sometimes they would sleep with statues of their deities beside them to try to inspire visions. The Ancient Greeks thought that Hypnos governed the realms of sleep, and through dreams brought messages to mortals from the pantheon of the gods. Rome accepted this belief when they adopted the Greek gods, and placed huge emphasis on dreamlore, with Emperors often paying seers huge sums of money to interpret their dreams.

Above: *The Romans thought that dreams held valuable secrets, and temples featured rooms where couples could pay to sleep in the hope of divine revelation.*

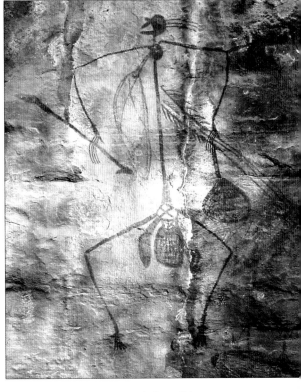

Left: This 15,000-year-old cave painting is thought to represent a sorcerer assuming the form of a stag. By imagining their quarry in dreams the tribal Shaman supposedly gained dominion over their prey.

At the heart of Aboriginal mythology is the Dreamtime. This was a time when sleeping spirits arose to create the world. They shaped the landscape, and brought into being all animals, plants and rocks by singing their secret names, before subsiding once again into sleep. Aborigines thus place huge significance upon the power of sleep and the messages it can impart. While the secrets of the Dreamtime remain concealed to all but a few tribal elders, images of it are often depicted in their rock paintings *(above)*.

Native American Indians also place great importance upon dreams, believing that sleep can reveal the hidden desires of the soul. They adhere to the belief that through dreams all creation and all the secrets of the world-of-man and the world-of-spirit can be revealed – and they select the person that shows the most proficiency in understanding dreamlore to be their Shaman. It is also through the power of dreams that braves are expected to gain mastery over the animals they track. Before a hunt they are expected to dream of the 'ways and language' of their quarry – thus developing an understanding and respect for a creature whose unfortunate but necessary death will be so important for the survival of the tribe.

FAMOUS DREAMERS AND DREAM INSPIRATION

Many musicians, artists, writers and inventors claim to have received inspiration through dreams. Our minds absorb a great deal of everyday information, both consciously and subconsciously, and the sleeping mind can often sift this information more effectively when the body is at rest. Although some of these ideas are too bizarre or extreme to be of any use, occasionally our sleeping mind interacts with a fertile imagination to inspire ideas which would never have surfaced during our waking life.

Perhaps the most profound work to be inspired by lucid dreaming was *Alice in Wonderland* by the Mathematician Charles Lutwidge Dodgeson (Lewis Carroll, *above*). Within its pages he successfully amalgamates the surreal elements of dreaming to create a book, not just about a dream, but about dreaming itself. Similarly, Mary Shelley claimed that the inspiration for her book *Frankenstein* was a dream she had after a conversation about the supernatural with her brother Percy Bysshe Shelley and Lord Byron. Although unlike Lewis Carroll's her idea was fully formed and

Far right: *The title page of Stevenson's first London edition of* The Strange Case of Dr Jekyll and Mr Hyde. *Richard Mansfield* **(right)** *was well known for his dual role in the stage adaptation – depicted here metamorphosing in this 1895 photographic double exposure.*

STRANGE CASE
OF
DR JEKYLL AND MR HY

BY

ROBERT LOUIS STEVENSON

LONDON
LONGMANS, GREEN, AND CO
1886

All rights reserved

Right: The Shakespeare Window in London's Southwark Cathedral – the Bard's works are scattered with allusions to sleep and the world of the dreamscape.

based directly upon the images she had envisioned in her dream – rather than the illusive and contradictory nature of dreaming itself.

Coleridge's *Kubla Khan* was inspired during an opium induced sleep. Upon waking he wrote 54 fully formed lines but was interrupted by a knock at the door and after answering it lost his inspiration.

The Spanish painter Salvador Dalí once claimed his work was a portrayal of reality seen through the subconscious rather than conscious mind, and thus he encapsulates the main elements of dreamlore in his paintings – depicting a land both distortedly surreal, yet hauntingly familiar.

Mozart also insisted that his best work came to him in dreams, while Giuseppe Tartini entitled one of his compositions *The Devil's Sonata* after remembering the notes played by the devil on a fiddle in one of his dreams. More recently, Paul McCartney wrote the entire song 'Yesterday' in one sitting, after waking from an unrecalled dream that left him feeling particularly inspired.

William Shakespeare often refers both directly and indirectly to dreams in his work and the influence they have upon his characters. *A Midsummer's Night Dream* is both a play about dreaming and an analogy of dreaming itself, depicting the confusion that can be caused during sleep. Some people also speculate that the pivotal scene in Hamlet – between the eponymous hero and his father – is in fact a dream, and is the Bard's warning to us never to take dreams at face value.

THE GREAT DREAM ANALYSTS

D reams are caused by the signals our minds send to our eyes at times of rapid eye movement (REM), which occur during sleep. Our brains trick us into believing that we are truly experiencing the visions we see before us by manipulating our visual and sensory stimuli. Whilst this scientific explanation reveals *how* we dream, we must look deeper for an understanding of *why* these messages are transmitted in the first place.

Current understanding suggests that dreams represent our memories – both conscious events we can recall and the subconscious images our brains absorb throughout our waking lives. We may think that the images we dream about are completely abstract but this is seldom, if ever, the case. They may be inspired by conversations we have overheard but not consciously registered. Images might pass by so quickly that our cognisant minds fail to 'apprehend' them – sights we have seen out of the corner of our eye, flickering pictures on a half-viewed screen, or people glimpsed through a crowd – all may find

their way into our sleeping mind. More often than not it is these nondescript fragments that resurface – yet it is not the visual recall but the emotion of the message that is of primary importance to the understanding of the dreamscape.

Sigmund Freud *(left)* is the best known of the great dream analysts. He stressed the crucial role of the subconscious in the shaping of our dreams, noting that dreams work on two levels – the 'manifest' or conscious, and the 'latent' or subconscious level. Dreams of sexual desire or violent intent are expressed in the subconscious, free from personal or social taboos. They represent wish fulfilment – which, he deduced, was most commonly expressed in adults by a lurid desire for sexual experimentation. Thus, he postulated that dream imagery is replete with phallic symbolism – represented by keys, rearing serpents, guns, and so on – or reference to carnal desire – such as dreams involving swimming, flying, or being impaled.

Alfred Adler *(below)* was a follower of Freud and introduced the theory of 'individual psychology' which stresses the importance of one's achievements and desires upon their dreams. Feelings of inadequacy in childhood will later be replaced by success-driven goals and elements of self-belief and self-doubt – it is the individual's desire for empowerment that most often shaped their dreamscape.

It was Carl Jung *(right)* who introduced the idea of the 'collective unconscious'. He believed that, along with

the personal input of the sleeper upon their dreams, there was a universal symbolic language which could be used to explain anyone's individual dreams regardless of their culture, religion or beliefs. Jung's work led to a closer evaluation of the symbolism of the dreamscape, rather than placing all emphasis on the individual's personality.

Jung's work was not universally accepted and amongst his detractors was Fritz Perls, founder of the Gestalt theory. He proposed that the characters envisioned in our dreams are merely depictions of our own personalities rather than collective images and it is us, and only us, that shape the course of our dreams.

THE SYMBOLISM
OF DREAMS

"Dreams and the visions of sleep are infused into men for their advantage and instruction." This was the view of Artemidorus, a Roman Soothsayer, and his words still ring true today. While each dream is unique to the individual, the collective importance of our dreams is to guide and instruct us. They reveal our innermost desires, our hopes, dreams and ambitions; though they also represent those cravings we may suppress in our waking lives, our fears and the stresses and strains placed upon us during waking hours. Dreams can be both positive or negative, and they universally serve to aid us in our lives.

The following pages present a collection of the most commonly encountered symbols that constitute the language of dreams, accompanied by explanatory text that provides the latest, most widely accepted interpretations of what these images mean.

DREAMING OF HOME

Home is important to us all. It is where we live, sleep and raise our families. Due to its place in all our lives it is hardly surprising that it plays such a prominent role in dreamlore. Houses have often been linked symbolically with the womb, representing a cocoon which no external factors can penetrate. In dreams they are the places we go to in times of insecurity and uncertainty – a shelter from all that threatens to overwhelm us.

To dream of being in one's home is a positive sign of comfort and internal security. However, when this image is disrupted by an alien image – anything from an intruder to a broken mug – it can be extremely unsettling. Such dream projections are the brain's way of telling us that there is something amiss in our waking lives. Most commonly these are small niggles such as overlooking a friend's birthday, or forgetting to put the rubbish out; but occasionally it is our mind's way of reminding us to do something positive for those within our family – perhaps visiting a parent, or spending time with a relative that we haven't seen for a while.

THE HOME OF YOUR DREAMS

E veryone has their own individual ideas of their dream home. For some it may be in the heart of a city *(right)*, for others it could be the back of beyond *(below)*. We are all individuals and as such have vastly differing needs and desires. These wishes hold special resonance in dreamlore and tell us as much about ourselves as people as they do about our home-loving aspirations.

The type of house that the dreamer chooses to inhabit within their dream is important. A country cottage may represent a desire to escape the worries and monotony of everyday life, and substitute the rat-race for a more leisurely existence. To dream of living in a palace or mansion could be considered a sign of pomposity and should be guarded against – this may not necessarily be excess pride in oneself, but may reflect misgivings you have about the lifestyles of others close to you.

Dreaming of a home in the city may demonstrate an innate desire for financial success, though how this is attained should be considered – for gains achieved by acrimonious means will invariably lead to misery. Country living is generally simpler, and illustrates the dreamer's desire for a solid family base.

Long winding roads leading to a house are a sign of positive advancement, though the longer they stretch, the more patient the dreamer may have to

be before achieving their goals. Country lanes that lead to your door prophesize travel or new beginnings, although muddy and rutted roads hint at a desire for isolation and tell of obstinate tendencies within the dreamer's character.

Dreamscape gardens also reflect the mind-set of the sleeper. Those who visualize coloured blooms and lush vegetation are invariably willing to work hard to achieve their success, while those with a garden given over to a vast expanse of lawn or paving are generally more impatient and may covet more immediate success rather than waiting for longer, harder earned gain.

Dreams of a childhood home generally display a simple longing for a return to an easier way of life. It is probable that you have several problems in your current life and you are yearning for a return to a simpler time.

Right: *Gardens are said to emphasize the female aspect of dreams; and nothing better illustrates this than 'In a Shoreham Garden' by the visionary artist Samuel Palmer, in which he pays homage to the spirit of Springtide fecundity.*

25

CROSSING THE THRESHOLD

I t is not merely the type or positioning of a home that is important in
dreamlore; all elements of the house – from the door to the décor –
have significance, and even outside features have their own resonance.

If a house is visualized with an open gate, the dreamer is inviting
opportunity into their life, and will probably be seeking to allow something
more spiritual into their lives. If the gate remains closed or is even locked,
this suggests that the sleeper is a guarded individual. This may be conscious
or subconscious, but usually indicates that they are stifling a relationship with
another person by refusing to let that individual get too close or involved.

Moving along the garden path we reach the door *(below)*, which is
representative of one's passage between particular states of mind or beliefs.
Numbers on doors can be important *(see page 184)* but it is the threshold itself
that is most significant. Crossing the entrance to a house has long been the
subject of superstition. Traditionally brides are carried across the threshold

of their marital homes as a gesture that the bridegroom will protect and provide for his spouse. Iron horseshoes placed above the door mantel are said to ward off evil spirits and grant protection against enchantment for those within.

If a door is seen to be locked or bolted *(above)* it represents a barrier through which only those with the key may pass. Freud viewed keys as symbols of sexual potency – with locks representing female sexuality – however, there are other dream interpretations; keys can symbolize the ability to unlock, or unpick, problems. Whoever is seen in a dream holding a key may also hold the answer to any dilemma the dreamer is currently struggling with. If the dreamer holds the key themselves, it suggests that given time and patience they can resolve their own problems.

Right: The medieval tradition of placing frightening figures on buildings to ward off evil spirits extended to more practical devices such as the door knocker. Gothic imagery invariably steeps into the dream-scape, where it may be regarded as a positive image with which to combat insecurity.

PROTECTIVE SYMBOLISM

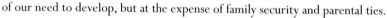

Our homes are often our first line of defence against the outside world; they make us feel safe and secure. Thus, when we see our homes destroyed or decaying in our dreams, it can feel extremely upsetting. However, these images do not foretell the actual destruction of our home, but are simply a reflection of our inner worries and concerns.

Destruction of a family home is a surprisingly common theme, especially among older children. Memories of our earliest homes represent the security offered by family bonds. As we develop, both emotionally and physically, we desire to move on, but also retain a fear of change. Images of our homes being destroyed are a subconscious acknowledgement of our need to develop, but at the expense of family security and parental ties.

Dreams of our family home on fire *(below)* may be representative of the anger we suppress when we are awake, and the acknowledgement that these

Dreaming of Home

emotions have the power to destroy that which we hold most dear. In dreamlore walls, unsurprisingly, are a sign of security and order. As in waking life they are seen to protect us from external concerns and help compartmentalize our feelings. When we dream of walls crumbling *(below)* or rotting away *(left)* it is usually a sign that we are anxious about a perceived loss of security or control. Dreams such as these are especially common at times of emotional upheaval, though they should not necessarily be considered ominous – sometimes in life we need to break down our emotional barriers in order to establish more lasting bonds of friendship or to expand and improve our personal lives, often at the expense of our own privacy.

Roofs are another symbol of shelter and security. A leaking roof may warn of a gradual draining away of our intellectual energy, and sensible steps should be instigated in waking life to improve matters. Stairs are talismanic of personal elevation – the implication of walking up or down steps is clear, but tripping on a step can be indicative of problems brought upon oneself. In particular it warns against meddling in the affairs of others where our motives may be selfish or self-serving – in such circumstances it is better for the sleeper to examine their true motives, and to act ethically.

THE HOME DREAMSCAPE

Different rooms in the house hold different connotations in dreamlore. At the top of the house the attic symbolizes intellect and curiosity. It mirrors the human mind, full of personal objects and thoughts that we may have discarded in our waking lives but which we revisit in our dreams.

Bedrooms characteristically represent security and rest, though they also hold sexual connotations. Small bedrooms may signify illicit feelings and secret desires, while larger rooms denote more open relationships which the dreamer feels comfortable to embrace.

Bathrooms in the dreamscape are synonomous with purification – and the washing away of past indiscretions. Clear water *(below)*, especially when used to clean the body, is a fortunate omen promising well earned reward, but dirty washing water foretells the shame of an unworthy action.

Living rooms or dining areas are at the heart of family life and symbolize our personal relations with others. If someone else is in the room their manner towards you is important. If they are hostile it suggests that you will experience problems with a lover or friend, but if they are welcoming this may herald the re-establishment of old acquaintances.

Kitchens are synonymous with domestication and may hold warm memories for the dreamer. A kitchen from one's childhood is a particularly cherished omen, speaking of a harmonious family life.

Right: In dreams our house is our inner sanctuary, but it is not unusual to find our worst imaginings — spiders, rats, snakes, etc. — inhabiting the dark corners of our home. These terrifying dreams are usually the psyche's method of exorcizing our personal phobias; by confronting nightmares we are better equipped to take control over them.

HOUSEHOLD OMENS

E ven everyday objects can offer a wealth of symbolism, and when exploring our dreams they should never be neglected. Furniture and utensils are important to our everyday life and, although we rarely consciously think about them, they appear with surprising regularity in our dreams to convey suptle and intriguing messages.

Candles *(below)* and lamps bring light into the darkness of our homes, and symbolize mankind's desire to illuminate our lives. In the Bible, candles and light are emblematic of spiritual

quest, and in many mythologies fire was the preserve of the gods before it was stolen by covetous man. In dreamlore light retains these religious and pagan connotations, and dreaming of a candle can symbolize a spark of inspiration that will deliver insight into a current spiritual dilemma or signpost the direction of possible solutions where none have previously been thought to exist.

Among the most familiar symbols in dreams are the cup *(right)* and bowl. Both are a reflection of our current outlook on life. If a cup is seen to be full it indicates that we are currently positive about our life – and heralds a time of self-created prosperity; however, if the cup is seen to be empty, the omens are reversed.

Chipped or cracked cups foretell small inconveniences that combine to drain our zest for life and create worry.

The appearance of scissors in dreams represents a fear of separation. They sometimes appear in the dreams of male adolescents, where they classicly symbolize an innate fear of castration. However, when related to the home, scissors represent a fear of being cut off from those whom we rely upon in everyday life.

Kettles *(right)* are closely associated with the hearth and retain this domestic relevance in dreamlore. To see a kettle boiling illustrates that current family problems will soon be at an end,

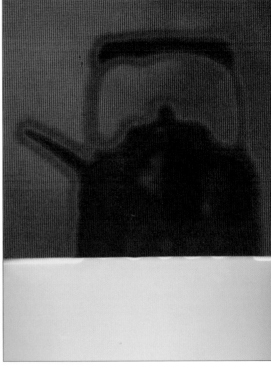

though if the kettle is dented and worn it may signify that there will be hard times ahead before things improve. If the sleeper visualizes holding the kettle, the omen relates not to their family, but to an improvement for themself. A steaming kettle reflects inner stress and anxiety, whilst an empty or broken kettle signifies a feeling of being alone or devoid of emotion.

Empty chairs *(opposite page)* indicate that optimistic patience is needed to achieve a long held ambition. If the chair is occupied by another person it may signal that the individual in question is currently 'standing in your shadow' – this does not mean that you need to cut them out of your life but, on the contrary, it illustrates a need to deal with the problems of others before your own. To view a chair pushed under a table signifies a brief but compelling relationship with an adventurous partner.

DREAM JOURNEYS

D reams of travel were once believed to be divinely inspired – a way of urging the sleeper to expand horizons (physically and spiritually) and make more of themselves. Thus, some mythical adventures begin with a dream vision, where a divine command would be given by a deity and a quest elected for the sleeper. To the Ancient Greeks, dreams of travel were extremely important and they would sometimes base expeditions to distant lands (and even campaigns against supposed enemies) upon the interpretation of dreams specially solicited by seers sleeping in designated dream-temples.

The transport we use for our dream journeys, the paths we travel and the experiences we encounter along the way are all important to understanding their meaning. Routes are rarely traversed with ease, and obstacles experienced relate to the difficulties faced in waking life. While pleasant scenery and easy paths forebode well, barren fields and rocky shores speak of lost direction. The people we encounter often have echoes in waking life, and arriving at a destination is an especially auspicious omen – hinting of goals that the sleeper has set for themselves.

THE ROAD AHEAD

In our dreams, as in our waking lives, we encounter many roads that must be travelled down to reach a destination, yet these roads represent more than simply a route from A to B. Instead they are symbolic of the decisions we all must make and the possibilities that lie open to us once our decision is taken. In dreamlore roads and paths represent the route to personal ambition. It may be short-term objectives, like promotion at work or getting fit; or longer term ambitions, such as commitment to marriage and raising a family.

Long, straight, roads are rare in the dreamscape, but if they do appear they signify that the dreamer will be able to achieve their aims easily if they have the right level of desire and choose to apply the correct level of effort. More common is a winding pathway or rambling country lane *(below)*; with each bend signifying a possible obstacle or pitfall that must be negotiated with due care and consideration – all will be well if you take 'one step at a time'.

Rocks and boulders may appear in dreams, strewn across the way, and representing small tasks that must nevertheless be completed. Paths that slope uphill signify struggle, while those that meander downhill might seem easier

to negotiate, but warn the sleeper against taking good times for granted.

Bridges *(above)* and tunnels link roads together, and in dreams illustrate the combining of two strands of one's life. They can also represent a social or

a business union, though if the bridge is seen to be weak or in danger of collapse, this should be taken as a sign that the dreamer should be wary that such a partnership does not erode long held ambitions.

Forks in the road *(right)* denote events that could divert you from your chosen path. If the road you select leads to a dead-end, it implies the dreamer has made a wrong choice in their waking life which they may need to re-evaluate. Crossroads hint that the sleeper has reached a stage in their life where an important decision must be made. In these dreams there is seldom an obvious route to choose – a direction may not necessarily be clear cut – so follow your intuition and remember that the best route is not always the one that appears the easiest to follow.

OVER LAND AND SEA

The type of transport that our subconscious mind chooses to utilize in a dream can be significant. Cycling *(below left)* is a cheap and convenient mode which requires a degree of effort to achieve results. In dreamscapes cycling

can prove an outward reflection of the dreamer's view of life – if they are constantly cycling uphill, this is a sign that they view life as a struggle and believe that rewards can only be achieved by hard work; conversely, a tendency to imagine cycling downhill illustrates a facet in the dreamer's personality to try and achieve the most they can out of life for minimum effort.

For many, most trips we make in waking life are by car, and these are thus likely to feature prominently in our dreams. To view yourself driving a car *(below)* is an affirmative omen and indicates a desire to take control of your own destiny – although to crash or veer out of control indicates you

are not as confident as you would like others to believe you are. Similarly, being driven in a car by another person – especially a parent or spouse – suggests that you currently rely far more on others than you may care to admit to yourself.

Trains, when dreamt about, indicate confidence and the belief in a rosy future; though to see a loved one leaving on a train signifies a current emotional distancing between them and you – the faster the train is seen to progress away from the sleeper, the harder it will be to rebuild the bonds of friendship.

Ships and boats *(below)* hark back to mankind's long fascination with the sea.

The wide expanse of the ocean stretching into the unknown promises the allure of adventure and excitement; and any form of transport that crosses it relates to a long held desire for independence.

Lighthouses *(above)* are dream harbingers of safety; they offer a beacon of light and, as such, illuminate a wise course of action in a sea of dark uncertainty. It urges the sleeper to listen to their instincts rather than be swayed by popular opinions.

INTO THE AIR... AND BEYOND

Mankind has always been fascinated by the prospect of flight. Flying is common in the dreamscape and unaided flight represents a desire to be free from the boundaries that we, or others, daily place upon ourselves.

While planes were still a new, and to many, a frightening concept, dreams of motorized air travel were considered unlucky. However, in today's world, where flying is a far more common occurrence, this view needs to be reassessed. To dream of piloting a plane *(left)* is an emphatic statement of self-confidence. It suggests that the dreamer has either discovered a new found belief in their own ability or they should give themselves greater credit for their recent achievements. To be a passenger on a plane suggests that you will receive good fortune, but through no apparent effort of your own. It is only when the dreamer visualizes a plane crash that negativity enters the dreamscape, hinting at possible setbacks. Such 'disaster' dreams invariably relate to the dreamer's emotions and not to likely waking events.

Thanks to technology, we are no longer restricted to our own world and can visualize travel to other galaxies *(far right)*. Dreams that explore the depths of space represent our psyche's desire to challenge our own preconceptions. Thus to travel in a space shuttle *(right)* reflects a desire for excitement and adventure. Yet for those that find such thoughts claustrophobic, the sleeping mind might well be prompting the dreamer to embrace the wider aspects of 'being' – to push forward their own boundaries.

CLASSIC TRAVEL SYMBOLISM

There are certain symbols that our mind intrinsically links with the notion of travel. These images regularly occur in dream journeys and each is redolent with meaning. The invention of the wheel revolutionized mankind's conception of transport, so there is little wonder that it is one of the first images that springs into our subconscious when we dream about travel. Wheels represent continuation – they are symbolic of the circle of life in which each season and component of the year is reflected by one of the spokes. In dreams the wheel also symbolizes home, where, no matter how far or fast one travels, like the wheel (that returns to its original position) we are always destined to return.

Above: The symbolism of the pagan 'circle of life' became grafted onto stories of christian saints, such as St Catherine.

Steps symbolize success either in social or financial matters. To be seen walking up a flight of stairs is a sign of achievement, whilst to walk down can be taken as a sign of failure

or simply the fear of over-stretching one's talents. Beware the step's condition
as slippery *(opposite below)* or dangerous treads, usually imply 'pride before a fall'.

Maps *(above)* denote order and precision. While they may represent travel,
they are more commonly linked to an inner desire to reorganize one's own life –
to put private affairs in order and to complete jobs that have long lain neglected. If
a map is confusing or unreadable it indicates a lack of self-discipline or motivation.
The compass, on the other hand, expresses a desire for self-improvement – though

it is the direction in which the needle points
that is the defining factor. East represents dawn
and youth, and hints at a need for the dreamer
to return to past values. West is symbolic of
sunset and rebirth – an omen of change. North is
supposedly connected to the soul and speaks of a
desire for spiritual enrichment, while finally, the
South is warm and exotic and foretells joy
in social relationships.

*Right: Despite changes to transport systems over the
years, our subconscious mind often clings to the nostalgic
imagery of childhood.*

TIME AND SPACE

Both time and space are human concepts used to explain and compartmentalize the rational world. However, our subconscious needs no such boundaries and can play with these concepts to rationalize the seemingly irrational – beings from other dimensions *(right)* can visit us and we can travel the universe. Days can disappear into seconds, while seconds can last lifetimes – all because our sleeping minds do not have to adhere to the same inflicted boundaries that our waking self must. Despite this lack of spatial and timely restraint, dreams of time and space have their own rationale which need interpretation.

Dreaming of the time of the day is relatively common, especially the dawn and dusk. Sunrise is representative of a fresh start and new opportunities for those willing to seize them, whilst sunset is more contemplative – the mind's attempt to reflect on past successes and failures to remind the dreamer of their own frailty and achievements.

Dreams of travelling through the infinity of space, which may be at once frightening and exciting, are also familiar to many sleepers; dreams such as these hint at changing circumstances and widening prospects.

THE ROUND OF THE YEAR

The seasons of the year remind us of the continuality of nature; just as spring follows winter, re-birth follows death. Life renews itself through circular progression, paying little heed to the linear time-frames set by man. Originally the Greeks and Arabs recognized just three seasons, spring,

summer and winter, which they correlated to the phases of the day – sunrise, noon and sunset. It was the Romans who introduced the fourth season of autumn, linking the year to the four ages of man, Spring, infancy; Summer, development; Autumn, maturity, and Winter, decrepitude. In dreamlore each season holds its own individual resonance, often closely connected to these ancient ideas.

Spring is the season of reawakening and rebirth and in dreamlore is closely linked to inspiration and the innocence of first love. To dream of a bright

Above: Hazel catkins are one of the first signs of the re-emergence of spring, telling us of nature's promise of a new dawn even in the depths of winter. To dream of catkins is a lucky portent which foretells increased fortune.

Dreams of TIME AND SPACE

spring day foretells new opportunities, especially for romance. Traditionally spring was also a time of departure, and in medieval times became closely linked with pilgrimage. Thus, spring can also represent the renewal of a quest, urging the dreamer to abandon the comfort zone of certainty to encompass new challenges.

The 'hazy, lazy mazy days of summer' are seen in dreamscape to represent 'wine of friendship'. If the dreamer envisages themselves relaxing in the sun with others it suggests strong bonds of friendship, or even love with one member of the group. Autumn, meanwhile, is the time of harvest – of stooked corn, ripened fruits *(above)* and glistening hedgerow berries *(right)* – in dreamlore this tells the sleeper to reap the rewards of that which they have sown, for unless success is celebrated it is destined to wither on the vine.

Since the ancients first linked the season of winter to death it has stood in our mind as the end, a full-stop in the story of our lives. However, nature does not subscribe to man's linear pattern of time, and its 'dancing circle of life' continues unabated. Winter *(left)* is thus a period of rest rather than of death, and in dreamlore a period of contemplation rather than despair.

WORLDS BEYOND

The question of whether we are alone in the universe is one that continues to fascinate mankind. Whatever the truth, we know that there are millions of planets in the universe other than our own. Our fascination with what lies beyond our own worldly confines means that other planets and stars *(right)* appear frequently in our dreams. The

ancients believed that our lives were guided by the stars. Emperors would pay huge sums of money to astrologers who they believed could foretell the future, and even today many still believe these celestial objects have influence over their lives. Dreaming of stars usually represents the sleeper's wish to control their fate – a single star appearing brighter than others represents a particularly auspicious development in the near future for the slumbering dreamer.

Our own star, the sun, gives us light and life, and its appearance in dreams reflects perception and a new understanding. This may mean the answer to a problem that has been vexing the dreamer, or a new opportunity to further one's learning. The moon is a feminine symbol that represents deep

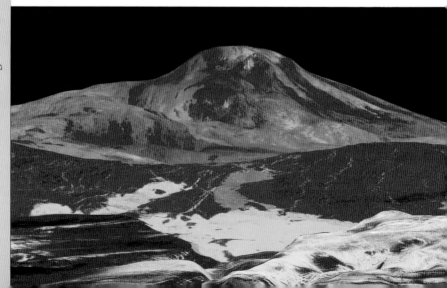

Dreams of TIME AND SPACE

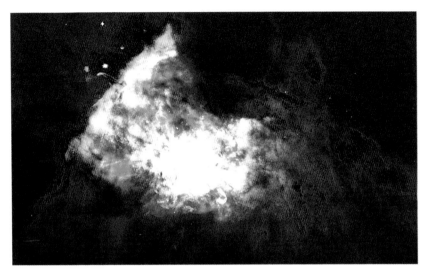

emotions and self-improvement. Its constantly changing nature and wandering across the night sky, was seen to reflect the shifting pattern of our own lives. An eclipse is considered an unfortunate event to view in sleep, as it suggests that a shadow may fall across the dreamer's path – though this may simply be a fear of the irrational which if dealt with soon can be easily resolved.

ELEMENTAL FORCES

The power of nature can be both wonderful and terrifying. From the delicate beauty of an individual snowflake to the tremendous power of a raging storm, nature has the ability to fill us with awe and wonder. In dreams elemental forces play a pivotal role, often directly mirroring the power of nature with extremes of emotions. Storms can foretell internal anxieties, while soft breezes indicate that the dreamer is at ease with themself.

The natural world is an unpredictable place and it has the power to change our lives, both for the better and for the worst. Natural disasters represent nature at its most destructive and it is little wonder therefore that the appearance of volcanoes, earthquakes, floods and droughts in our dreams evoke such powerful emotions.

The Ancients believed that the world was comprised of the four elements of water, fire, earth and air – each holding its own meaning within the realm of dreams. Although today our view of the world is more complex, these four elements still play a vital role in the nature of elemental forces and, as such, upon our sleeping minds.

WEATHER LORE

Rain is often seen as an inconvenience, yet it is essential for the growth of plant life. It was commonly viewed as a pagan symbol of fertility, and even today rain is seen as a sign of divine blessing in drought affected regions. In dreamlore rain is a lucky omen. To dream of being caught out in the rain is considered a sign of joyous fortune. A gentle shower symbolizes good grace and improved luck. Similarly, sunshine is also considered a fortunate element within the dreamscape and represents the easing of personal problems.

Rainbows have long been seen as a symbol of the divine. After the great biblical flood, God sealed his promise to Noah – that never again would he allow such an event to occur – with a rainbow. In other religions, the arc of a rainbow is seen as spanning the divide between our world and the heavens, and in dreamlore it retains this sense of divine providence. Rainbows have many dream interpretations, from travel or unexpected good news, to requited love and insight into one's own spiritual persona.

Rime – frozen water vapour upon winter trees – can transform a familiar scene into one of enchanting mystery *(left)*. Its sunlit sparkle and soft, silent shimmer evoke magical images. However, its ghostly appearance spells disaster for newly emergent crops and its presence in dreams sits uneasily upon the dreamscape, where it forewarns the sleeper not to claim success for a venture until the rewards have safely been achieved. Similarly, frost warns against promises that can easily be broken; though the appearance of icicles *(right)* implies that you are in danger of appearing emotionally cold and need to show more warmth.

Mist *(above)* and fog are invariably thought of as mysterious and eerie. They are usually a sign that the dreamer is trying to conceal something in their waking life. Often this is a guilty secret kept from others, but may also represent the sleeper's waking mind attempting to hide their own true feelings from themselves.

THE FOUR ELEMENTS

It was once thought that everything in the world could be divided into the four elements of Water, Air, Fire and Earth *(opposite page)*. Although such notions no longer play a significant role in our view of creation, they continue to retain much of their potency and importance within dreamlore.

Water is essential to life, both practically and spiritually. In most religions there are stories of healing waters, and in Christian baptism it is still considered by many a necessary step in one's communion with God. In the dreamscape water is commonly regarded as a precursor of good fortune, athough there are notable exceptions – spilling water denotes a quarrel, and to view one's reflection warns against placing too much gravitas upon our own opinions.

In ancient philosophy, it was believed that the body's vital energies were carried in, and thus represented by, the element of air. This has led to links with our physical wellbeing. To dream of warm air cautions against the possible onset of a self-inflicted illness, whilst to imagine cold air blowing against the body suggests a reflection upon the suitability of a current tryst.

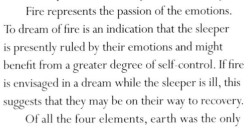

Fire represents the passion of the emotions. To dream of fire is an indication that the sleeper is presently ruled by their emotions and might benefit from a greater degree of self-control. If fire is envisaged in a dream while the sleeper is ill, this suggests that they may be on their way to recovery.

Of all the four elements, earth was the only one considered to belong, not to the gods, but to man. It is a practical element that when viewed in dreams implies a rise in status – from a position of scorn to one of honour.

Left: To imagine that a wind blows in a dream often enhances the surreal nature of the dreamscape, adding an element of unease – the greater the wind's force the more potent the symbolic omens are considered to be.

THE RAGING EARTH

While the earth is full of beauty and wonder, the power of nature should never be underestimated. When pushed to extremes the earth can react with frightening ferocity. Volcanoes *(below left)*, earthquakes, floods and hurricanes all cause widespread devastation and it is little wonder that such catastrophes in our waking lives evoke uncomfortable symbolism to our sleeping mind. Throughout history, despite the danger they pose, people have lived on the edges of volcanoes benefiting from their fertile soils. Eruptions are usually rare occurrences, and in dreams it is the smouldering volcano that may be evoked *(below right)*. This represents the repression of emotions that threaten to 'explode.' Often this pent-up passion is linked with unfulfilled carnal desires, but this frustration can just as easily represent jealousy or envy. These feelings should be treated with care and addressed during waking hours, so as not to consume us.

Tidal waves may sweep away all that lies within their path. In dreams they represent strong emotions that threaten to 'sweep you off your feet' – although they can represent the cleansing of the dreamer of defunct ideas and self-defeating feelings. Drought *(above right)* is an omen of misfortune.

It may signify that you are putting a lot of effort into a venture which will produce little reward or that you are emotionally investing in someone who is unlikely to return your feelings. On a more positive note, however, such dreams will prepare the sleeper for similar pitfalls in the future.

Although floods can be extremely destructive, in dreamlore they have more fertile connotations. The prosperity of Egypt was built on the Nile's annual flood, and just as the Biblical flood cleansed the world of sin, in dreams they have come to represent the end of an old way of life and the beginning of a new one. Similarly, earthquakes are disruptive to dream about. In ancient times it was believed that they spoke of war and turmoil. Today they are seen to be closely linked to upheaval in our personal lives.

EARTHLY TREASURES

The natural world abounds with a wide variety of objects we regard as treasures – from the metallic beauty of gold and silver, to the organic perfection of pearls and amber; nature holds many wonders which we desire to claim as our own. From the dawn of the earliest civilizations, mankind has coveted these natural riches and they have been used as symbols of status ever since. Today our world would not function without them. Gold still forms the basis of our financial system, just as it did when King Croesus of Lydia first struck gold coins nearly three thousand years ago.

Dreaming of precious stones and metallic treasures is often believed to foretell financial reward; however, this is seldom the case. In fact, the more earthly treasures you accumulate in a dream generally implies the less your materialistic gain is likely to be. Those who dream of finding treasure may discover improvements in their social life or romantic prospects, rather than in their bank balance. Although this apparent reversal of fortune may disappoint some dreamers, it should be remembered that wealth is transient, whereas emotional riches, health and contentment far outweigh financial reward.

PRECIOUS METALS

In today's society gold and silver are generally considered to be among the most precious metals. However, metal has a more serious purpose than mere surface appearance. Less valuable metals such as iron, tin and copper are vital in our daily lives, and as such enter the realms of our dreams.

In both Eastern and Western tradition, gold *(below)* was often seen as the encapsulation of the power of the sun in solidified form. Because of this, and due to its rarity, gold was used to make important objects, both for religious, magisterial and social purposes. Unlike most metals, gold will not rust, so it was seen as pure and incorruptible. In dreamlore gold is closely associated with honour and success – it delivers the 'shining prizes'.

While gold encapsulates the masculine power of the sun, silver is linked to 'Sister Moon' and has become closely associated with female spirituality. It is used to symbolize chastity and eloquence, but due to Christian tradition – where 'thirty pieces of silver' became tainted by Judas's betrayal of Christ – the metal is now indelibly linked to falsehood. In dreams it is said to act as a warning against the shortcomings of others, especially untrustworthy friends.

Generally dreams of metal represent the sleeper's own 'cold' or 'hard' qualities and suggests they would benefit from a more relaxed approach to life;

however, specific metals also have their own individual meanings. Copper objects signify unfounded worries, brass represents emotional strength, zinc indicates substantial and energetic progress, and lead warns against lethargy and placing too much reliance upon the good will of others. Iron was once considered the 'metal of the gods'. In many religions it held a magical quality and was commonly used to fashion talismans. Even today a horseshoe is viewed as a lucky symbol (dating back to when iron horseshoes were hung over doors to ward off evil spirits). Iron appears in dreams as a sign denoting personal success and empowerment; however, the presence of rust upon iron (above) reverses the omens – if rust is seen on a surface it denotes romantic problems, while to get the metallic stain upon your fingers indicates failure of a cherished goal.

Above: To dream of molten metal foretells that your impatience will court failure; however, just as smelting removes impurities from metal ore, to dream of a foundry suggests redemption.

ORGANIC TREASURES

Some precious objects are not made by geological processes but by living organisms. These treasures – notably pearls, ivory and amber – are often just as prized as their metallic counterparts, and are just as talismanic in dreamlore. Pearls *(below)* are particularly poignant, as they represent hidden beauty. Just as a pearl is constituted from the irritant of a grain of sand into a thing of beauty, to dream of one suggests that love may be found in the most unlikely places, and with a person the dreamer would not readily consider.

Amber, a fossilized resin produced by pine trees, was often used in amulets because of its supposed magical qualities. It was called 'the tears of Heliades' (a sun nymph) by the Greeks and 'the tears of Freya' (a Norse goddess after whom Friday is named) by the Vikings, and was thought to be a part of the sun fallen to earth – as a shooting star. Its presence in dreams denotes balance and harmony within the sleeper and hints of an inner wisdom and spiritual enlightenment.

Ivory *(right)* was once prized even more highly than gold. However, unlike gold (which can be re-smelted) ivory remains unchangeable when carved, and has echoes in the dreamscape, where it signifies continuity and longevity. In the 17th century Sir Thomas Browne stated that all dreams passed through one of two gates – one made of ivory and the other of horn. The dreams that passed through the gate of horn would prove to be delusional, but those that passed through the gate of ivory would come true. Old almanacs warn those who dream of ivory to beware the acquisition of easy wealth through hunches or through investing in risky ventures. Today, the circumstances in which ivory is obtained greatly compromise it as an omen.

ADDING SPARKLE TO SLEEP

Dreams of EARTHLY TREASURES

The beauty of the earth is encapsulated in the gems *(right)* it produces. As such these jewels are regarded as highly prized treasures. Dreaming of finding any precious stone is a positive sign. Like fairytales we may sometimes envisage treasure being guarded by dragons or other mystical beasts; this symbolism is conjured up by the subconscious mind to illustrate, not merely the importance we place upon such riches, but also the subliminal feelings that treasures should be earned by hard graft *(below)* rather than simply taken when stumbled upon. However, rarely do riches in dreams signify material wealth; more often they denote physical or spiritual quests and attainments.

Of all the precious stones, diamonds are the most valued. They are the hardest of any known substance and can only be cut by themselves – thus diamonds symbolize permanence and incorruptibility. Other precious stones are closely linked to our emotions. Rubies – greatly revered in the Middle Ages as a cure-all for plague and poisoning – denote passion and the enslavement of desire. Sapphires, with their shimmering blue tint, embody

the virtues of resilience and truth. Emeralds, once believed to be the solidified form of serpent venom, have poisonous portent for those who dream of the green jewel – said to induce envy in those who view it in sleep. Amethysts, topaz and lapis lazuli all warn the dreamer to beware the dangers of intoxication, unchecked desire and pride respectively.

Gems are most commonly seen during dreams, as in waking life, as adornments – necklaces foretell

the accumulation of wealth, bracelets indicate the spread of gossip about you, whilst for a sailor to dream of an earring supposedly forecasts a watery death by drowning.

Right: *We have called upon the earth's riches to create works of art that range in diversity from the earliest Neolithic brass bangles to contemporary jewellery design. Here the natural world merges with that of dreams, as the artist pays homage to nature in gold, citrines and yellow sapphires.*

DREAMS OF LANDSCAPES

From the highest mountain to the lowest valley, from the deepest ocean to the smallest stream, dreams of the natural world serve to remind us of nature's beauty. However, dreams about the landscape do more than just highlight the natural splendour we all too frequently take for granted – they emphasize elements of our lives by illustrating our current physical, spiritual or emotional wellbeing in the symbolism of our surroundings.

Forests are harbingers of hardship and frustration, in which vegetation conspires in our downfall; mountains represent achievement and a desire to strive towards success, while water (including rivers, lakes and oceans) is strongly linked with our emotions. Views of gently rolling hills and fertile fields *(inset)* evoke in us a sense of wellbeing and comfort. Ploughed fields herald success won through hard work, whilst rambling hedgerows and meandering country paths invite opportunity.

Dreams of destroying the landscape are symbolic of the destruction of elements within ourselves. This may suggest we are denying our true emotions in our waking life, or that we have sold our integrity for personal gain.

LUSH FORESTS AND ARID WASTES

Trees embody life and growth and were once considered to represent the union of the three realms of earth, heaven and water. Even today in some parts of Africa trees are worshipped, while in China trees planted in the vicinity of ancient tombs are believed to house the spirits of the dead.

In medieval times much of Europe was covered by forest. Living in the open, cultivated land, men began to associate the woods with darkness and chaos. Elements of forest folklore remain in people's minds today, and

psychologists associate dreams of the 'wild wood' with deep-seated problems and hidden emotional baggage.

Dreams of forests and woods have come to represent feelings of unease with one's life. To imagine being lost in a forest denotes that the sleeper feels overcome by the pressures of everyday life; this is usually closely linked to financial matters, but can also represent feelings of social isolation or lack of personal direction. These dreams can be further complicated by the appearance of thorns and briars *(above left)* which conspire to ensnare the sleeper and prevent them from moving forward. A forest fire *(below, centre)*

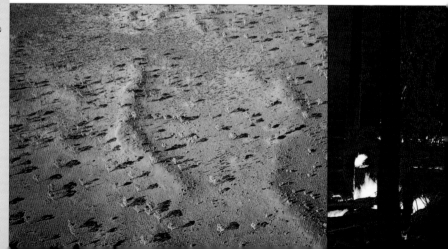

may further endanger the dream traveller within the landscape, and underlines the powerful message the subconscious seeks to deliver.

Jungles and rainforests *(left)* hold similar connotations to forests, although they have the added dangers of deadly animals and poisonous plants. In this context the appearance of a snake represents a rival to another's affections, while vines and creepers warn the dreamer not to become too emotionally involved (or entangled) in a relationship.

Deserts *(below, left and right)* are hard unforgiving environments where life struggles to survive. The arid waste of the desert has come to symbolize troubled times in the dreamer's life, and their need to rely on others to help them through. However, if the sleeper stumbles upon an oasis in the middle of their 'desert', this should be viewed as a talisman of renewed hope – the promise of closure to a period of uncertainty in the dreamer's waking life.

'THROUGH HOLLOW LANDS AND HILLY LANDS...'

From mountain to valley – the 'hilly lands' and 'hollow lands' of Yeats' 'Song of the Wandering Aengus' represent fertile ground for dreamers. Mountains are considered the place where heaven and earth met – where attempts to reach the peak are treated more like pilgrimages than a mere expedition to the summit. While mountains may have lost their direct religious connotation, they still symbolize aspiration and the search for higher meaning.

For those that stand at its foot, a mountain represents obstacles to be conquered. Similarly, mountains denote troubles in the dreamer's life that they may feel are impossible to overcome, or a task that appears almost impossible. However daunting it may appear, the dreamer will usually find that if they start their climb it is not as hard as they expected. To imagine oneself climbing the mountain *(below)* is a sign of advancement – of social or spiritual maturity. To reach the summit is symbolic of a deep personal achievement and the pride you will feel once your waking goal is achieved.

While mountains represent the ferocity of the elements and the unconquerable power of nature, valleys are seen as welcoming and habitable. They are places where mankind can settle, and have strong links to raising families. To dream of a fertile valley with an abundance of flora and fauna foretells successful parenthood, while barren valleys imply family troubles.

A valley shrouded in darkness or engulfed by mist indicates problems in a relationship. If there is a stream in the valley the speed of the water indicates the dreamer's mood; if the river is clear and fast-moving they are positive about the future, but if it is sluggish and meandering the challenge faced is harsh.

RIVERS, LAKES AND STREAMS

Rivers and streams were the life source of ancient civilizations. Not only did they need rivers to carry goods between settlements, but the Egyptians relied upon the Nile's annual flood – the gift of Isis –to water their crops and ensure survival. In dreamlore flowing water symbolizes our life-force. Clear, swift currents indicate health and success, while shallow, brackish water heralds possible stagnation and indecision.

Lakes *(below)* indicate our mood. A placid surface unfurrowed by ripples and movement suggests contentment with life, while stormy waters denote that the dreamer is troubled by negative emotions that should be addressed. To see moonlight reflected in the surface of a lake suggests the sleeper is becoming emotionally involved with a partner who shares their intensity of feeling. However, to view oneself drowning suggests that the dreamer is being overwhelmed by conflicting emotions and needs to 'take a few steps back'.

Dreams of Landscapes

Rivers represent the dreamer's lifespan. Fast flowing water suggests a carefree attitude to life and a desire to embrace all it has to offer; while a meandering river full of bends *(below)* implies the dreamer is plodding through life with little direction and even less enthusiasm. To dream of crossing a river is an indication that the sleeper has a decision to make. The degree of difficulty they experience in crossing – slippery banks, fast moving currents and the depth of the water – will serve to indicate how hard this choice will be.

Waterfalls *(above)* are a fortuitous omen, though they come with an implicit warning. To see a waterfall in a dream means the sleeper may achieve their deepest desire. However, if they view themselves endangered by the power of the falls, they may find that their wish does not bring as much pleasure as once assumed.

Small streams can represent creativity. To bathe in their waters is a sign of a desire – to embrace your talent and to use it to full advantage. However, an unwillingness to submerge may illustrate that the dreamer is reluctant to use their creative skills to full capacity.

THE SEAS AND WIDE OCEAN

Despite their size, in dreamlore, seas and oceans retain the link between water and our emotions. Calm seas are a sign of inner contentment while stormy oceans represent turmoil and troubled times ahead.

Many dreams of the ocean can be linked to feelings of love, though rarely are they positive. Dreaming of crossing an ocean may represent a romantic challenge, although the progress and condition of the vessel you envisage to complete the ocean crossing is important –if it flounders this is a discouraging omen… worse still if it sinks! To dream of waves breaking on the shore forebodes an argument, while to hear the distant sigh of the sea upon a reef is considered a sign to reflect well upon choices to be made in waking life.

Despite negative omens, many dreams of the sea may be viewed as life affirming. To dream of wading in a clear blue ocean signifies confidence in your own ability; swimming in the sea is a sign of 'washing away' your worries; while dreaming of diving in illustrates a wonderfully relaxed spirit.

For many, to imagine that they are underwater is a familiar dream theme — cut off from the rest of the world, and in a spiritually uplifting environment, it is pure escapism. The most common setting for such dreams is a coral reef *(left)* where the experience is heightened by a mirage of ever changing colours and shapes. Dreams such as these are an escape from worldly troubles, and provide us with a much needed break from the stresses of life. However, they can hint at our inability to face real situations and the need in our waking lives to overcome our problems before they overwhelm us.

Dreaming of ocean breakers pounding upon a rocky coastline *(above)*, hints of the dreamer's inability to make coherent decisions in their waking life — each wave represents an unsolved problem crashing down upon the sleeper, and wearing away at them.

To dream of a desert island may seem idyllic, but commonly represents a sense of boredom in the dreamer's realm. The less there is to do the greater the sleeper's lethargy. Wet sand from the beach upon our skin *(above right)* can be an irritant and serves to remind us not to be complacent in our lives, but to embrace all we have and to be grateful for it.

PLANTS AND FLOWERS

Plants are the very embodiment of Mother Nature. They feed us, heal us and decorate our homes. Throughout history people have used plants both for their own purposes and in the worship of their gods. Even today they hold many important religious connotations. Mistletoe and holly decorate homes at Christmas, and yew trees are still planted in churchyards where their bright, waxy berries remain a symbol of remembrance.

The frequency with which we dream about flowers and plants is testimony to the hold they exert within dreamlore. Strong feelings are engendered by them. If we are content, we may dream of sitting in a summer's garden surrounded by dazzling flowers, but if sad or confused we may dream we are lost in the darkness of a vast forest.

The close connection between plants and nature means that when they do appear in dreams they are often associated with strong natural desires. These may be positive (roses symbolize love and affection) or negative – where withered and dead flowers denote disappointment. But, however they appear, plants and flowers serve to remind us of the world's beauty, and the role we must play in preserving it.

DREAM FLOWERS

Flowers evoke powerful images in our conscious and unconscious mind; we associate them with strong feelings and transfer these to our dreamscape. Roses are regarded as flowers of love, and in dreamlore they retain this symbolic link. It used to be believed that if a woman dreamt of picking roses, she would awake to an offer of marriage. Today we realize that this quaint belief is too simplistic a notion, yet to dream of receiving the 'Queen of Flowers' still remains a symbol of a strong physical or spiritual attachment to a current partner or friend. As a sign of female sexuality, the rose is said to awaken our earliest prenatal memories – the pink or scarlet petal-head resembling a long vanished echo of the enclosing womb.

In Christian iconography, the lily has close links with the Virgin Mary. Its white petals were commonly spread on the bed of newly-weds to symbolize the virginal purity of the bride. However, in dreamlore the lily carries a mixed message of sadness tinged with joy.

The colour of flowers has its own dream iconography. To see white flowers in sleep indicates purity and the transcendent; yellow blooms are linked to wealth and majesty, but, by extension, envy; red is indicative of passion and sexual chemistry, whilst purple and mauve flowers (*right*) denote chastity and feminine spirituality.

Left: Wild orchids are said to represent animal passion. Their vivid colours and phallic shapes symbolize wantonness and debauchery. To dream of orchids denotes a lustful encounter, while to see them wilted portends sexual frustration. This example of a bee orchid is well chosen, as the plant's velvety flowerheads serve to lure bees to its pollen receptors by the ruse of sexual deception.

Dreams of PLANTS AND FLOWERS

78

WILD FLOWERS

Wild flowers are intimately connected to the seasons. They often last but a few weeks before succumbing to the 'round of the year'. They swim before the eye with colour to represent the vibrancy of nature, yet in their fragility is forecast the inevitability of their passing. Thus, to dream of walking in a field of wildflowers is suggestive of youth and vitality, but because of their impermanence they caution the dreamer to 'seize the hour'.

Individual wildflowers have their own specific meanings. Poppies *(top right)* are one of the plants most closely linked with sleep. Morphine, extracted from poppy seeds, derives its name from the Roman god Morpheus who was thought to help promote sleep – the vivid red of the petals was claimed to induce vivid dreaming. In the realms of sleep the poppy is often viewed with a certain hopeful trepidation and seen as a symbol of fleeting happiness; just as a poppy when picked will soon wilt and die, these flowers presage a brief romance, albeit one filled with tenderness and love.

The primrose is amongst the most beautifully delicate of wildflowers and it symbolizes eternal love, comfort and peace; it is often found in country churchyards growing on the graves of lost loved ones. Cowslips promise

success in the workplace and strong bonds of friendship, whilst violets speak of joyous occasions and matrimonial devotion. Buttercups, dandelions and daisies are common flowers of our fields and meadows, yet are often overlooked by many; their presence in dreamlore signifies the many small blessings we can all too easily take for granted.

Forget-me-nots are dream heralds of love and hope. They supposedly get their name from the legend of a medieval knight and his lady, who were sitting beside a fast flowing river when the knight gathered a bouquet of bright blue flowers to give to his sweetheart. As he reached for the last one he lost his footing, slipped into the river and was swept away. Ever since they have symbolized everlasting love, and in dreamlore they underlie the strong bonds of fidelity to a current partner, or deep feelings for someone from your past that you will never forget.

Above: *In dreamlore the harebell is a sign of sacrifice. Once thought to be unlucky, today we view it as a symbol of reward following hardship.*

CROPS AND HARVEST

Crops have always been a matter of concern and celebration for mankind. Even today in many parts of the world a good harvest means the difference between life and death. With this in mind it is little wonder that crops and their successful harvesting remains an important focus of our sleeping as well as waking lives.

Although for most of us a safe 'harvest home' is no longer a prime concern, many of us dream about Mother Earth in some shape or form. Crops have always been closely linked to the gods, and it is they who were thought to dictate how abundant the harvests will be. This link to pastoral fortune has been maintained through our subconscious, thus to envisage a plentyful harvest is said to portend success for an important venture.

In Ancient Greece, corn *(below)* was believed to be the offspring of the sun and the earth, and was considered symbolic of both fertility and divine wisdom. In dream almanacs it was closely linked with emotional fulfilment as well as financial reward. Wheat holds close connections with loving partnerships, and even more auspiciously, the fertility of an enlightened mind.

Vineyards and orchards represent long life and prosperity, though to see yourself picking the fruit is sometimes regarded as an unfavourable omen and warns of hardship through folly. This may be linked to the myth of Persephone, who had to spend six months every year in the Underworld – one for each of the pomegranate seeds she ate from the fruit offered to her by Hades.

Hops *(left)* are closely linked to sleep. Many natural sleep-inducing remedies include hops, and their presence in the recipe are said to inspire sweet dreams. They are among the most magical and mysterious of all plants, whose properties one suspects are yet to be fully realized.

To dream of sowing seeds implies a period of personal hardship that will ultimately result in prosperity. To view one's self gathering in the harvest foretells success won after struggle. Despite the apparent advantages of dreaming of reaping that which you have sown, a degree of caution needs to be recommended – any acquisition of personal gain should be tempered with magnanimity, lest it be taken for granted and ultimately wasted.

Right: To dream of an orchard clothed in springtide blossom presages the success of an ambition. To imagine one hanging heavy with ripe fruit points to the consolation that years of hard toil will not pass by unrewarded.

TALISMANIC PLANTS

Trees hold important religious significance. In the Jewish Cabbala the sephiroth tree of life is seen to link heaven and earth, and this image of an 'earth tree' is repeated in Norse, Roman and Greek mythology. Trees have always been blessed with talismanic qualities and, as such, command respect within the dreamscape – inviting us to reach for the heavens, whilst ensuring we keep both feet firmly planted on solid ground.

To see a tree in your dreams is generally a happy omen that portends the fulfilment of one's hopes and aspirations. If the dreamer climbs a tree this is symbolic of swift advancement; however, to imagine becoming enmeshed in a tangle of roots at the base of the trunk is redolent of our basest earthly desires.

The oak is known for its strength, and it is commonly believed that to dream of one whilst pregnant will herald the birth of a strong, healthy baby. However, it is also said to be talismanic in the devotion of love. In Medieval England it was believed that placing an acorn *(bottom right)* under a maiden's pillow would cause them to dream of their future husband.

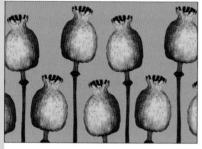

The ash tree *(opposite page)* and the hazel bush were both considered sacred in Celtic mythology, and today reach us in folk-echoes that speak of the joy of the intellect – in particular the Celtic delight in the use of language and the juxtaposition of word-play. Similarly, hawthorn is said to ease the passage of speech. Yew is a tree whose presence in a dream emphasizes gravitas and a need for careful consideration if new ventures are to be undertaken or fresh plans made.

Seed heads *(above)*, seeds *(centre right)* and fruits have a myriad of meaning within sleep. Rowan berries *(top right)* once protected against witchcraft, and today their scarlet fruits are said to guard against trickery and deception. Sloes *(middle right)* from the blackthorn bush may look appetizing, but they have a sour taste to metaphorically warn the dreamer about taking things at face value.

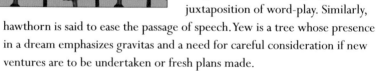

PRICKLES, POISONERS AND STINGS

Not all plants are content to be mere objects of decorative adoration; some have no intention of simply 'looking pretty', but instead have developed intricate ways to defend themselves. These plants are viewed by many with distrust and even scorn, but their place in dreamlore ranks alongside their more attractive cousins. For example, unlike the edible mushroom, toadstools are often seen as the harbingers of poisonous intentions. Their vivid colours and bold shapes warn against their lethal flesh. When encountered in dreams – usually as the fairytale form with red tops with white spots *(below left)* – they act as a warning against unhealthy desires or the pursuit of vainglorious pleasure. If they are seen to be eaten, their meaning is even more sinister, foretelling degradation and disgrace.

The poisonous plant mistletoe holds deep mystical connections. Ancient druids believed that because it grows high above the ground it was divinely favoured by their gods. Mistletoe had to be picked extremely carefully, because it was thought that if the gatherer allowed the plant to touch the earth they would evoke the wrath of the heavens. Its highly potent berries were used as a powerful toxin. Today

Left: *In dreams the cacti's thorns warn against small differences of opinion that might lead to a much larger rift.*
Below: *Deadly nightshade's poisonous berries contain the dream warning to beware those of our acquaintance who present themselves in an attractive fashion, but whose actions have more sinister intentions.*

it is more closely associated with the iconography of Christmas, and mistletoe is considered a lucky plant to kiss beneath. In dreamlore it heralds fecundity and sexual potency, and to dream of presenting a lover with a mistletoe bough suggests the strengthening of important bonds of romance and friendship.

Brambles, nettles *(above left)* and teasels *(below right)* are often seen in dreams blocking our paths. These represent troubles and misfortune, though they should not be viewed with alarm – they are not signs of ills to come, but a suggestion to try to solve the problems in our waking life.

Right: *Beauty beguiles… once the rose has become a scarlet hip the vicious nature of its tangled web of thorns emerges into view.*

87

ANIMAL VISITATIONS

A nimals have long been regarded as possessing an insight into the natural world that mankind has lost. Thus dreams featuring animals often hark back to a primeval longing for a simpler existence.

Animals play an important role in our waking lives, so it is only natural that they feature prominently in our dreamscape. From time immemorial animals have been closely connected with the gods. From Ancient Egypt to Christianity, from the 'Dreamtime' of the Aborigine to Islam, animals have performed a central role in shaping our spirituality. Even in the modern world animals are intrinsically linked with abstract concepts. Our subconscious immediately connects lions with courage, dogs with loyalty and ants and bees with relentless toil and labour. It is these links that begin to help us to understand the messages they bring to our world of sleep.

A whole spectrum of different creatures may appear in our dreams, helping us to understand our own subconscious minds. Some act as omens of good fortune whilst others forebode ambiguous luck. However, all of them illustrate the importance that the animal world still has in our day-to-day lives.

THE CALL OF THE WILD

W ild animals represent some of the most exciting dream images because we associate them with a sense of danger. The lion is one of the most powerful animals in both nature and symbolism. Throughout history the lion has been coupled to the concept of power and might. After Hercules slew the fearsome Nemean Lion, he wore its skin as a sign of strength. Medieval kings demonstrated their might by adopting the lion as a heraldic symbol of power – the most famous being Richard I of England, nicknamed the 'Lionhearted'. In dreams, a placid lion denotes personal gain, but if the lion is angered the omen is reversed and it means possible loss.

The tiger (*right*) is another fearsome animal of dreamlore. William Blake's 'dread beast' the Tyger is seldom an easy bedfellow, and those who are stalked by tigers in their dreams should guard themselves against dangers lurking just out of view. If you run from the beast it means that you fail to confront your problems, but those who stand up to the beast should take encouragement, as it indicates that resolve and determination will eventually prevail when troubles seem to surround you.

Another favourite beast of our dreams, the elephant, is known for its longevity and powers of memory. For this reason if encountered in a dream it is considered a talisman of business acumen and innovation.

Left: *Caged animals traditionally represent the death of innocence – that harsh reality will soon intrude upon an idealistic situation. The cage may also be symbolic of a sense of repression. To find oneself trapped means that the dreamer feels they are suppressed by emotions which need to be confronted – although to escape from the cage shows an ability to move towards the freedom of a less constricted and regulated life.*

FRIENDS TO MAN

Domestic animals hold different connotations to those of wild creatures. They are an important part in our lives, and thus command a special place in modern dreamlore. Horses and ponies (*right*) represent the qualities of nobility, speed and power. In the Middle Ages a horse signified valour, whilst to the ancient Celts they were symbols of primal energy – often becoming the tribal totum. In dreams they represent elements of arguably the most primal of all energies – love. To see a horse running free foretells a passionate affair, whilst to dream of riding bareback indicates a desire to be overwhelmed. However, to be thrown from a horse is not an auspicious omen and may well indicate that 'love offered' will be 'love scorned'.

In most cultures dogs (*below right*) have been seen as embodying the important qualities of loyalty and steadfast courage. In dreams they symbolize

a desire to balance approval with integrity. To the Celts, dogs were symbols of healing, and if a dreamer envisions a dog licking a wound it is thought to portend (however unhygenically) the curing of an ill – either physical or mental.

Cats, meanwhile, have a tainted historic pedigree. Whilst in Far Eastern

cultures they are often viewed with reverence, in the West they were associated with fickleness, poverty

Left: A cat riding a dog shows how dream images often intermingle to produce surreal images that appear normal during sleep, but are bizarre once we wake.

and, as his 'familiar' even the Devil. To dream of a cat can represent a warning of treachery and double dealings; however, it can also be seen as signalling an independent spirit and a desire to break free from orthodox constraints.

Like cats, pigs have often suffered from a bad reputation. Invariably seen as dirty and lazy, I much prefer Churchill's insight 'that a dog looks up to man, a cat looks down at man, but only a pig can look you in the eyes as an equal'. In dreamlore they are thought to portend fortitude and hope against the odds.

Otters (*right*) illustrate well how attitudes to animals change over time. Once considered a pest for the part they played in depleting fish stocks in rivers, otters are now viewed as friendly, lovable creatures. To dream of one is a sure sign of encouragement, and reflects the dreamer's playful *laissez-faire* attitude towards life and living.

SEA CREATURES

Images of deep water represent profound, often subconscious, thoughts; thus those creatures that live in this silent domain are intrinsically linked with such ideas. Crabs *(right)* have thick shells and fierce claws, and warn those that dream of them to beware of anyone who uses bravado and threats to get what they want. To imagine an octopus *(below)* may also represent a difficult, but eventually rewarding, outcome to a persistent problem; if only the dreamer has the tenacity to grapple with the problem they will eventually find a solution.

Fish are considered harbingers of inspiration and creativity. It used to be thought that dreaming of a fish would lead to wealth, though this is certainly not as clear cut as was once believed. Some fish — especially salmon and trout — symbolize esoteric wisdom long lost to mortal man; they are often represented as spirit guides in Celtic myths and legends. To dream of catching fish denotes the pursuit of wealth, which may just as easily slip from your grasp. Different parts of a fish can hold different connotations — to dream of a fish's eye demonstrates an astute, watchful nature, whilst fish scales illustrate a desire to feel protected at any price and whatever the implications may be.

To dream of a fish out of water struggling for breath, not unnaturally, denotes that the sleeper feels overwhelmed by problems, or has recently been placed in a situation where they feel uncomfortable. However, a fish that has been caught but escapes to the water illustrates fortitude to overcome one's problems.

Dolphins (*above*) are sea creatures beloved by man. They are perceived as friendly animals, rumoured to help those in trouble at sea. In dreamlore their presence symbolizes the emotional attachment of the psyche – their interest in us (swimming towards us, or darting away out of sight) serves to differentiate between the profound and the superficial.

Whales (*right*) are no longer the feared 'monsters of the deep' they once were assumed to be. Now these gentle leviathans are viewed as symbols of peace and inner strength. In the biblical tale of Jonah, the whale represents the jaws of Hell from which the sinner can only escape through supplication to God. Similarly, in dreams, the whale represents the 'womb of nature' from which we may begin a spiritual journey of rebirth. They warn of inner struggles, but also of a better life to come after these troubles have been acknowledged and vanquished.

ENEMIES IN THE SHADOWS

To dream of a creature that we may fear or loath in our waking lives is far from a portent of bad tidings. Creatures that terrify our conscious minds have much more colourful and positive subliminal meanings. The classic example of this is the snake (*below*). While some people still argue that snakes denote loss, sacrifice and ill fortune, this biblical view ignores their greater symbolic meaning. In Norse mythology 'Ouroboros' (a snake swallowing its own tale) represented the circle of life; whilst in Greek and Egyptian mythology, two snakes entwined was symbolic of the healing power of nature. In dreams snakes represent regeneration and renewal – just as a snake sheds its skin, so too will the dreamer discard elements of an old life and start anew.

Like snakes, crocodiles (*above right*) and alligators are often vilified. These creatures were important in Ancient Egypt, where they were

occasionally mummified along with the Pharaohs. Whilst they represent brutality, evil and treachery (all traits of the Egyptian crocodile god Sebek), they are also linked in dreamlore to strength and hidden character. To envision a crocodile may represent possible danger lurking beneath the surface – perhaps friends that are not all they seem to be, or colleagues that seek to advance themselves at your personal expense.

For many, spiders are something of a nightmare, but in dreams their influence is far less terrifying. In Native American tradition they are seen as creatures of deep intelligence and prosperity. Dream-spiders often appear when the sleeper needs to make an important decision. They can also denote tremendous tenacity in pursuing an objective. Webs represent home life and the ability to understand and heal family rifts. Bizarrely, it was once believed that if you dreamed of swallowing a spider you would awake with a magical way with words.

Left: To dream of snakes used to be seen as a portent of evil. Today, however, it is generally believed that snakes can signify the beginning of a new way of life.

FEATHERED MESSENGERS

Birds are prominent and powerful symbols within the dreamscape. Throughout history they have shared a strong symbolic connection with the gods, either directly as their messengers or as portents of their will.

Flight is often seen as signifying freedom from the restrictions that tie us to earth, hence birds often represent breaking away from the ties of an old life in search of a new. To encounter a bird in flight in a dream may be considered an elevating experience leading to greater independence in both thought and deed. However, to come across a bird in a cage means that the dreamer feels restricted or held back by some aspect of their waking lives; they literally need liberating from the imprisonment of their current circumstances.

To dream of brightly coloured birds represents the wish of the sleeper for a more exciting lifestyle – as exemplified by dream images of the flamboyant peacock (*above*) or the spectacle of massed flamingos (*below*). Such magnificently plumaged birds can also act as a warning against the dangers of vanity and self-aggrandizement.

Nests are symbolic of home life. To see a nest containing eggs may mean additions to your family, although not necessarily the birth of a child.

Left: Kingfishers offer optimistic omens, promising good luck for those that are fortunate enough to dream of them.
Below: *In dreamlore birds such as the bee eater (that incessantly dart about, seemingly in every direction), signify that the dreamer's path through life has many directions that the sleeper may be compelled by circumstance to follow.*

However, if you see a smashed egg, or if you smash an egg in your dream by mistake, it may mean a family argument is brewing, or that you are neglecting someone whose love is important to you. A deserted nest is always a sorrowful omen and may indicate that you are worried about the loss or absence of a good friend.

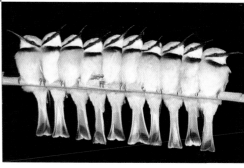

Eggs, themselves, hold a significant place in dreamlore. They play a role in the cycle of creation, and symbolically represent a life renewed. In the world of dreams eggs may mean a search or a quest – this may be an external challenge the dreamer is facing, or even a sign that they are struggling internally. It can also denote that they have dormant talents that they are yet to discover.

THE DREAMLORE OF BIRDS

Different birds have different meanings within dreams. Surprisingly, one of the most auspicious of all birds is the ungainly pelican, which acts as a symbol of self-sacrifice and is often associated with the suffering of Christ. In times of want the pelican was believed to feed its chicks on its own flesh to keep them from starving. In dreamlore the 'pelican in its piety' is a symbol of self-sacrifice and may appear when the dreamer has important decisions to make – which involve them putting the needs of others before themselves.

Conversely, the cuckoo (*right*) is the antithesis of the pelican. In nature the cuckoo foists its eggs upon other unsuspecting birds, and thus to dream of a cuckoo implies deception. While this deception may come from an external force – forewarning of problems in a loving relationship – it may also be motivated by the sleeper's own jealousy and misunderstanding. Thus it is important to explore one's own conscience before accusing others.

The Owl (*below*) is one of nature's most fascinating birds. Owls were closely associated with the gods. Athena, the Greek goddess of Wisdom (who herself

has a close connection with the realm of dreams) used an owl to communicate with mortals on earth. Their eerie screeching and silent, ghostly flight have, over time, tarnished them with an unfair representation as harbingers of death. However, in dreams owls are now believed to represent the need of the sleeper to seek advice from an older and wiser source, and to place reliance upon their years of experience.

Crows and ravens hold a similar association with 'black legends.' Considered once to be birds of ill-omen, because of their prominence on battle-fields pecking at the slain, they later became associated with witchcraft and the black arts. Their presence in dreams often suggests betrayal or abandonment; however, due to their mystical role as the 'eyes of Odin' – chief of the Norse gods who surrendered an eye in exchange for the power to look into the future – ravens and crows now represent the power of foresight.

The dove is a worldwide emblem of peace, and in dreamlore it offers similar omens – signifying that the sleeper's worries have been over exaggerated or unfounded.

Right: Dreams involving pelicans draw on a deep well of metaphor. The birds were believed to love their chicks so much that they fed them on their own blood. In dreams they stand for the noble virtue of self-sacrifice.

UNLOVED AND UNWELCOMED!

Animals that we may at first disregard as unimportant (partly because we'd rather not think of them at all) actually appear in our dreams with surprising regularity. Their place in our imagination is tarnished by association and reputation, but this does not diminish their role in the pantheon of the dreamscape.

In life flies (*right*) are seen just as a petty annoyance, but in dreams they can forecast greater problems. Flies signify disturbance to the pattern of everyday life. If they are seen as a swarm this suggests that the dreamer is being overwhelmed by problems. Rats and mice offer less sinister omens and invariably signify news. Dreaming of a rodent standing on its hind legs looking at you heralds the arrival of important information, whilst to see one scurrying away indicates that the dreamer is having vital facts denied to them.

Toads (*below*) were associated with witchcraft, and it was once supposed that toads had a secret jewel hidden within their head. Today we know this not to be true, but its place in dreamlore remains – you should look for the true character in someone (good or bad) and not be fooled by first impressions.

Right: *Although the link between fleas and diseases such as the Black Death was not known until centuries later, fleas were seen as 'the devil's creatures.' In dreams they symbolize seemingly small problems that may do more damage than expected.*

Dreams of ANIMAL VISITATIONS

CREATURES OF THE DUST

Creatures that scurry in the dust or swarm through our dreams may seem to be of little consequence, but they are more important than we imagine. Dreaming of a swarm of small animals signifies that individual vexations, that alone could have been easily dealt with, have multiplied to such an extent that they now threaten to overwhelm you. However, if a swarm is seen dispersing this is a sign that the sleeper can overcome their problems by dealing with them in a methodical manner, issue by issue.

While butterflies (*right*) symbolize rebirth and the dreamer's desire to progress, caterpillars and grubs (*below*) hold more ominous connotations. They suggest that the sleeper will mix, or is mixing, with uncouth and base people that will seek to drag them down to their own level. Moths also hold a darker symbolism. To envisage a moth in flight warns against the rashness of letting your heart rule your head, whilst to see a moth dancing around a light or flame clearly warns against the rashness of sexual indiscretion.

Left: *Caterpillars can be joyous omens of an improved life, suggesting that just as the caterpillar emerges as a butterfly, we too can become better people.*

Above: *To dream of a butterfly flitting from one flower to another is a delightful omen of freedom – try to learn from the emotional responses your psyche evoked.*

Ants are well known symbols of hard work, which achieve their goals through social enterprise rather than individual effort. For those who dream of these industrious insects they foretell the promise of a successful business or a mutual venture. If the ants are seen in a great number, this success will be even greater.

In Ancient Egypt the scarab beetle was a symbol of the sun and resurrection. Amulets depicting beetles were worn as signs of good luck. While in dreams the Scarab beetle is generally viewed as a symbol of good fortune, other beetles are not so positive. If the sleeper dreams they are covered in beetles this suggests that they have a great number of problems that they feel they cannot resolve. To envision being bitten by a beetle symbolizes that there is someone, or something, vying for your attention that you are currently ignoring.

STINGERS AND SWARMERS

Dreams in which you are stung symbolize the pain you have caused others, or will cause someone through your misdeeds. Wasps are the most likely agents of a sting, and to dream of them forewarns you that gossip may be being spread about you by people you trust. Dreams in which a hornet appears signal serious disruption in a friendship or some sort of complication in a financial transaction.

Bees have religious connotations. In medieval society they were considered to be both intelligent and mysterious, and were nicknamed 'the birds of God'. In Islamic belief Mohammed is said to have allowed bees to enter heaven

Above: An illustration of bees leaving the hive from a 14th century manuscript. The insects were regarded as divine messengers, and in dreamlore their actions should always be heeded.

because they represented the people's souls. This positive lore reflects itself in dreams, where bees are seen as a symbol of happiness. Their hard work suggests that those who dream of bees will find success in whatever venture they undertake. To see bees making honey (especially in an orchard) offers the implication of financial reward. However, if you dream of killing a bee it supposedly heralds the loss of a close friendship, or a lover parted by jealousy.

Mosquitoes in dreams represent people who, in your waking life, are trying to get all they can from you without giving anything in return – literally, 'blood suckers'. Scorpions are extremely potent for their size. In dreamlore they symbolize unforeseen problems that have been allowed to enlarge out of all proportion. Similarly, if a scorpion is seen with its stinger raised ready to attack (*right*), this suggests that the sleeper is keeping a dark secret that is about to rebound and 'sting' them.

ABOUT OURSELVES

....

" We are such stuff as dreams are made on." Nowhere does this quote from William Shakespeare ring more true than in dreamlore. Our sleeping thoughts revolve around us, and therefore we – ourselves – are always the most important subject of our own dream. Thus, the symbolism of our physical bodies and the mental image we have of ourselves is vital to interpretation.

Most people think they know their body well, and so it seems surprising then that we rarely appear in our dreams as we imagine we do in waking life. We often envisage ourselves less attractive or thinner than we are in reality, or with bigger muscles or firmer breasts. This self-image is a reflection of how we desire to be seen – but is not necessarily how others perceive us. While most would benefit from a little more exercise, or taking better care of themselves, we must remember that friends and family invariably love us for the way we are, and that change should be for our own benefit and not merely to conform to any perceived social stereotype.

CALLED INTO BEING

Many women dream of being pregnant. Even females who do not yet wish to have babies, or who may not want children at all, will invariably find that they experience this dream at some point in their lives. This could be due to the natural maternal instincts conditioned by the brain, which during sleep are uninhibited by the rationale of waking factors. For some, dreams of pregnancy may be simple wish fulfilment, a desire to have children or to start a family. For others however, the dream simply prophesizes new beginnings – a new start to a particular period of your life, perhaps the start of a new project or scheme that had been constantly put off, but which can now at last begin.

More surprisingly perhaps is the frequency with which men dream about being pregnant. Some experts have suggested that this is a longing to reconnect with the 'child within', although more feasibly it appears (as for

Babies *(left)* signify our sleeping minds' need for nurture and care. They can express our desires to raise children, but for some dreamers it signifies a suppressed wish to return to a simpler time when a parent controlled our problems and worries. Dreaming of suckling milk further underlines this desire to escape from current problems by retreating to a time of innocence. To dream of holding a baby's hand *(below)* is perhaps one of the most poignant we can visualize, yet the question must be asked – do we hold a younger version of ourself?

women) to be a paternal awakening – expressing the desire to start a family and raise children. When prompted, dreams such as these can provoke powerful emotional responses, and may be the psyche's prompt that life could have more to offer you than you currently appreciate.

Dreams of birth often seem to be linked to spirituality and increased creativity. Healthy babies, easily delivered, imply that the dreamer will discover a new talent previously unknown to them. If the labour is perceived to be difficult the sleeper may expect to encounter problems along this path of self-discovery.

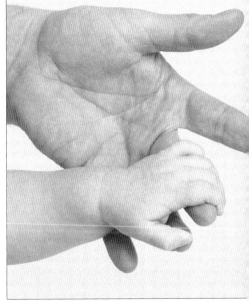

THE FACE

O ur faces are the part of ourselves that most clearly display the emotions we feel. When we are happy we smile, when we are sad we cry and when we are confused we frown. In dreams our facial expressions, as well as those of others, encompass a wealth of visual symbolism.

To see the face of a friend or relative, especially someone recently deceased, could signify the communication of a message. This is seldom spoken, and the

clues to what they are trying to impart are in their expression. If they are smiling this may be taken as a sign that they are pleased with you, or want you to know that they themselves have found contentment. If they are sad or angry they may be trying to express their displeasure at some unworthy action.

Eyes have been described as the 'windows to the soul', and some people believe that their colour reflects a person's true character. This imagery is mirrored in dreamlore, in which blue eyes suggest fickleness and warn of inconsistency in love. Hazel eyes tell the dreamer to beware those who would use flattery to deceive, and brown eyes caution against placing too much faith in what is 'said' as opposed to what is actually 'done'. The 'all seeing eye' (*above,* as it appears on a dollar bill) has often been used to denote the omnipotence of God. To see it in a dream cautions the sleeper against dishonourable actions, telling the dreamer that even when they think they are acting in an 'up front' and reasonable manner, their conscience will always be there to judge their actions; the sleeper may be able to justify self-interest in the waking world, but their subconscious mind is not so easily fooled.

Dreams of ears or mouths reflect concerns the dreamer may have that others are talking about them behind their back. An open mouth can signify the onset of an argument, a laughing mouth foretells reckless behaviour, and a closed mouth with luscious lips indicates sexual desire. Decaying teeth (a common theme) represent fears for one's health, while losing teeth suggests anxiety at the prospect of growing old.

BODY LORE

I n dreams we often see ourselves not as we are in reality, but as how we would ideally like to appear. Despite these differences in perception there are common features in dreamlore and the realms of sleep that relate to all our bodies, whether they be large or thin, tall or short.

The neck is seen as a bridge connecting the intellect of the head to the strength of the body, and its appearance in dreams warns the sleeper to use their head (signifying 'reason') as well as their heart in matters of love, and not to throw themselves blindly into a relationship without first considering the repercussions. Shoulders represent a burden which we are happy to accept, and which will give us a new perspective on life. Backs are viewed with slight suspicion, as in waking life we cannot turn around to see our own back, thus in dreamlore they tend to hold connections to the unknown. To envisage your back in a dream implies that others may be plotting against you,

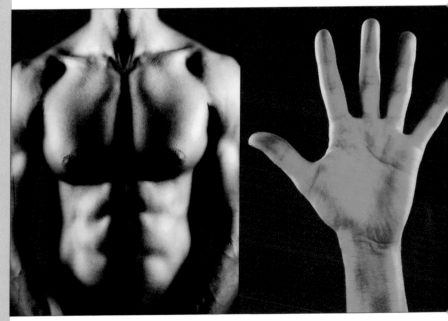

Dreams ABOUT OURSELVES

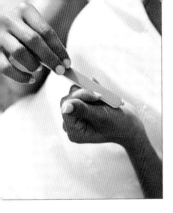

whilst to view someone turn their back to you indicates loss of prestige and influence.

The chest is an area representative of strength and authority. To imagine you have a powerful torso is a sign of empowerment for men, whilst women who dream of their own breasts are considered to be confident and high achievers – the bigger their chest appears, the more auspicious the omens! This echoes the time of the Pharoahs, who believed women with large breasts possessed an intuition that others lacked.

The visualization of legs and feet in a dream symbolize the foundation and basis of the sense of stability in our lives. They imply the sleeper will achieve their ambitions through hard work – literally by 'finding their own feet' and will make the most of whatever opportunities present themselves. Dreams of nails *(above)* imply a suspicious mind that will seldom receive a present without suspecting that trickery or an attempt to deceive is the real motive for the gift.

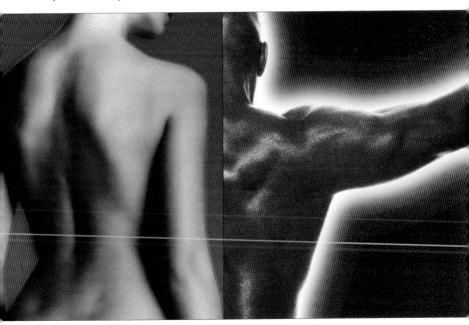

WHAT LIES WITHIN

A lthough we usually pay more attention to our physical appearance than to our inner self, it is what is contained beneath the surface of our skin that is essential to our daily wellbeing. While we may rarely consider this aspect of 'self' in our waking lives, our internal organs, muscles and fluids may occasionally be represented in our dreams.

The largest of all human organs is the skin. Dreams in which the sleeper is keenly aware of the sensual nature of their skin *(below)* show a perceptive prowess which will serve the dreamer well if they are forced to rely upon their own intuition and the viability of quickly formed judgements. To see yourself shedding your own skin demonstrates that you are changing as a person – often involving a loss of previously held inhibitions.

Dreaming of organs of the body relates to our physical wellbeing. The stomach is an indicator of emotional, as well as physical, health – with the stress of the waking world often causing imagined stomach aches in the realms of sleep. To dream of the stomach may suggest digestive problems but more commonly is a reflection of the worries in waking life. Dreaming

of the liver may imply a need to detoxify our bodies or change our diets; lungs, said to be linked to the soul, reflect concerns we have about lost spirituality.

The heart is one of the body's most important organs and in dreamlore represents sincerity and compassion. Due to its connection with romance, some have claimed that its presence in a dream heralds the start of a new romance or the rekindling of a previous one. Muscles *(above)* suggest the latent strength of the body and symbolize hard work and toil. The skeleton represents mortality – 'all things to end are made'– and demonstrates an acceptance of one's own mortality, showing that the dreamer is comfortable with their life at present.

Blood is representative of our life force and is held sacred by many religions. To bleed in a dream symbolizes a loss of power.

Right: *Microscopes scrutinize in minute detail, and to visualize one in a dream cautions the sleeper that by reading too much into one particular aspect of a situation they may lose the wider perspective.*

LIFE'S LITTLE IMPERFECTIONS

There are very few people who are completely happy within their own skin. For most we may regularly worry about our appearance – do we have too many spots?... are we losing our hair? Dreams frequently take these concerns and exaggerate them, or even imply conditions we do not have. These little imperfections are subconscious reflections of our fears, but they also tell us more about the way we live our lives than we often realize.

Freckles, spots or blemishes may commonly be visualized in dreams, especially for those going through puberty. Often we exaggerate their importance in our waking lives, and in our dreams they reflect this inflated anxiety, telling us that we are making too much of trifling worries.

Many of us fear losing our hair. In dreamlore thinning hair can represent financial loss for men, but conversely implies success in a woman's career. This may be partly due to the sad Victorian belief that if a women lost her hair she would have to make her own living in the world because no man would marry her. For both sexes hair-loss also warns against excess vanity. Going grey signifies maturity and an increased knowledge; whilst finding hair growing in inappropriate places, not unsurprisingly, forebodes social embarrassment.

Dreams of growing fat are sometimes taken to be a positive sign of increased prosperity, yet they could just as easily demonstrate worries for your health and fitness – if you are concerned by what the scales indicate *(left)* try to instigate remedial action. Dreaming of being thin may be interpreted as a sign of loss and hard times ahead. To age in a dream means that you will make wise and informed decisions, while to become significantly younger suggests that you are currently acting with a reckless disregard for the facts.

118

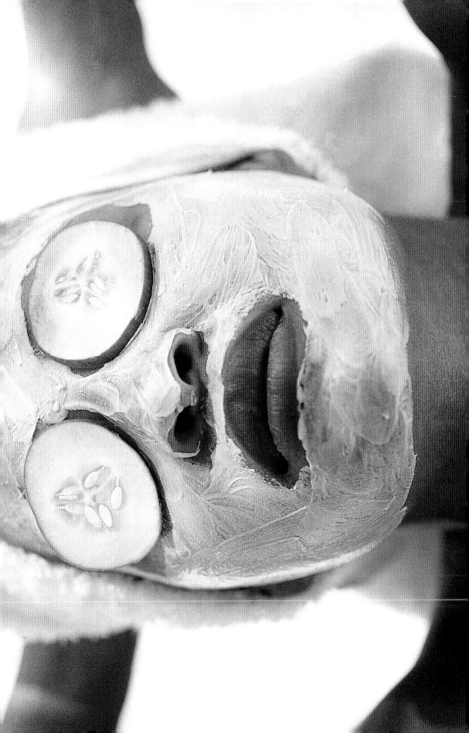

UPON REFLECTION

Naturally we tend to place ourselves at the centre of our dreams, though we rarely appear as we imagine. Sometimes our physical features are altered for the better or for worse, sometimes we see images of ourself through the eyes of others.

Fear of embarrassment often dictates the way we behave during our waking lives, and dreams where we embarrass ourselves can be unsettling. Two of the most common dreams of imagined humiliation are undressing in public *(right)* or finding oneself naked in a public place. While these dreams may seem cruel on the surface, they are often just the mind's way of unburdening repressed anxieties,

often forged during childhood, which have been allowed to fester and multiply over time.

Shadows *(left)* are rare in dreams where the rules that dictate our waking lives seldom apply. While Jung argued that the shadow can be interpreted as an extension of 'self', the ancients viewed it as a separate entity – an omen to be wary of. Because of this longstanding notion of mistrust, on the rare occasions our shadows make an appearance in a dream they signify self-inflicted shame.

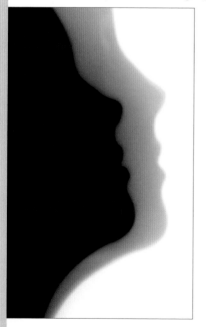

Footprints left in the snow or sand can act as guidance, and the dreamer should pay attention to where they lead. If the prints are made by the dreamer, it forebodes a period of confusion.

Right: *In sleep your psyche can take you to any destination. To visualize a footprint (as here, on the lunar surface) confirms your arrival somewhere. Be sure to remember the location, for, exciting or dull, it may reflect opportunities offered up to you in waking life.*

In our dreams mirrors seldom reflect how we really look, but beguile or flatter the sleeper as their vanity dictates. As a general rule you can interpret a mirror dream by simply reversing its apparent meaning. To dream of a cracked mirror presages overheard gossip that the sleeper will not want to hear.

LIFE AND DEATH

Our health, and that of our friends and family, is one of our greatest concerns and this worry permeates our dreams. Visions of sickness and hurt are never pleasant, though they should not always be considered ill omens. In fact, such images usually serve to help us, highlighting problems we might ignore in our waking lives.

The Greek doctor Hippocrates, the 'Father of Medicine', believed that dreams could help the healing process. Even today there are people that claim we can cure ourselves through the power of our dreams. While there is little direct link between our dreams and our physical wellbeing, sleep is an important part of any healing process and, due to the optimistic attitude it gives them, those that experience positive dreams may often recover more quickly.

While dreams of illness very rarely portend poor health, if you have recurring dreams about a specific area of your body, it may be advisable to consult a doctor. Although rare, during restful sleep well away from the stresses and strains of waking life, your brain can occasionally highlight problems that your waking mind may have missed or overlooked.

DREAMS OF ILLNESS AND INFIRMITY

Dreams of illness and infirmity can be greatly unsettling, but while they appear to foretell ill health this is, in reality, rarely the case. Often such dreams merely seek to highlight our inner fears and concerns, or warn us of dangers which if acted upon can be avoided.

In dreams where the sleeper appears to be hurt, it is important to take note, not of the condition that the dreamer is suffering from, but the pain itself. If the pain is light it may suggest that the sleeper will have to suffer a small degree of discomfort – occasionally physical, but more often emotional or spiritual – to achieve a planned goal. However, if the pain is intense, the dreamer should re-assess whether these plans are worth the heavy price they will have to pay to achieve them.

Dreams in which your body feels tired or strained are a sign that you are taking life too seriously and that you need to relax before the best of life passes you by. Fevers and fits symbolize that you are worrying unnecessarily over trivial matters and need to re-assess your priorities. Dreaming that you are insane highlights feelings of helplessness and an inability to deal with the problems in your waking life – in such cases it may be advisable to seek the support of your family in order to help bring these troubled times to a swift conclusion.

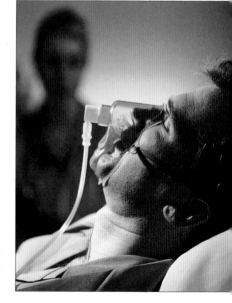

Right: *Dreams of dying can be unsettling, but they serve to warn us that we are threatened from an external force. This may be a rival who undermines us at work, a rival in love, or even someone who drains us of our emotional life-force.*

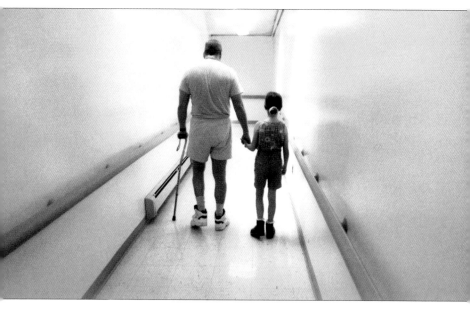

Dreams of impotence may be common amongst men, and illustrate a fear of not being able to compare favourably with a partner's previous lover – which in itself can engender anything from mild annoyance to a sense of total helplessness.

To dream of having a disability suggests that there is something lacking in the sleeper's waking life. If the dreamer imagines they are blind, it may denote that they have lost sight of their ambitions and long to recapture the drive they once had. If they dream they are deaf it could suggest that the sleeper has become too focused on their own needs at the expense of others. If they imagine themselves to be lame or to have lost the use of their limbs *(above)* they seek attention and companionship. However, it must be remembered that some dreams of paralysis are simply caused by trapping a nerve uncomfortably during sleep.

Unseen accidents are all the more shocking for their unexpectedness. Although they are rarely omens of actual misfortune they serve to focus our minds on the questions we rarely like to ask ourselves – 'what if something really did happen to me?' Such dreams remind us to confront our own mortality – to make a will for example – or prepare other seemingly distasteful preparations.

DOCTORS AND NURSES

D ue to the role they play in helping cure us in our waking lives, in our dreams doctors *(below)* are viewed as positive omens. To see oneself visiting a doctor is a sign that any minor problems the dreamer is experiencing in their lives will soon be settled. To meet a doctor in a social capacity is auspicious, suggesting good health and prosperity. If a doctor comes to your home it indicates that friends and family will rally round you to help sort out any problems you currently experience. If the sleeper imagines that they are gravely ill, it is usually taken as a sign that they remain healthy in waking life – an example of the subconscious mind's 'contrary thought' where anxieties are dealt with by the expediency of imagining a worst-case scenario.

To dream of a psychiatrist indicates the sleeper may feel threatened by external forces, but surgeons denote support by their guidance and support.

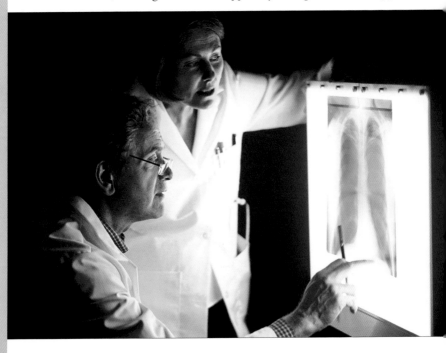

Like doctors, nurses can be viewed as encouraging figures within dreamlore. If they are viewed holding a baby or a small child it should be taken as a sign that the dreamer will enjoy a new and rewarding friendship. If a nurse is seen entering or leaving the house it is usually a portent of balanced health. A woman who dreams that she studies medicine to become a doctor may reflect that she is held in high esteem by her fellow workers, who value the rewards of her efforts and achievement.

To dream of taking medicine *(above)* may leave a bitter taste in your mouth, but ironically the more bitter it tastes the more fortuitous the omens will be. The idea that 'what tastes bad must be doing some good' applies in dreamlore – implying that hard, onerous effort will eventually be seen to bring reward.

Left: Dreaming of taking pills illustrates that you may doubt your own abilities, and place reliance upon formulaic remedy. However, the dream implications suggest that you are the only person to question your prowess – have more faith in your own abilities and start using your skills to help yourself and others.

'IT'S FOR YOUR OWN GOOD!'

Noneof us like the idea of injections, or going into hospital to have an
operation, but we appreciate that it is for our own good. Dreams
of things we might be scared of, but which we know will help us in the long
run, invariably contain messages for our own good. We might not want to
hear them, yet they improve our lives as well as those of others.

Many people have a phobia of hospitals and simply dreaming of them can
make the sleeper feel uncomfortable and anxious. Their appearance in our
dreams may seem unlucky, because they might imply that a friend or family
member will face a traumatic time; however, rather than being harbingers
of gloom, such dreams serve to remind us of our obligations towards others.
By spending more time with those we love, listening to their problems and
supporting them, we can assist them in overcoming difficulties – whilst at the
same time helping ourselves to become more empathetic and understanding.

Operations *(below)* are seldom to be relished. In dreamlore seeing oneself
being operated upon is a sign that the sleeper needs to take stock of their life

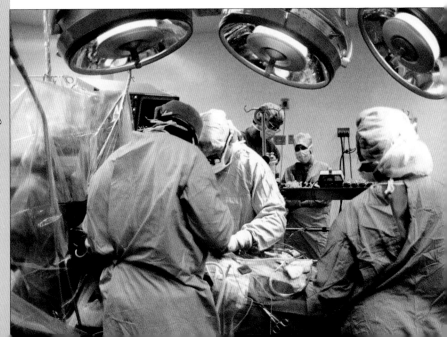

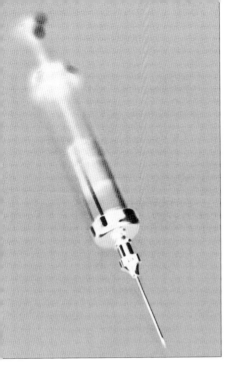

Left: Hypodermic syringes are one of the most feared medical images and, just as the pain we expect is often more intense than the reality, in dreamlore they suggest the idea that we may currently be blowing small problems out of all proportion – learn to suffer a little for the greater 'whole'.

and reassess their priorities… are you spending too much time at work?… have you been neglecting your family?… have you lost sight of your childhood goals? All these questions and more need to be addressed and answered. While truthful responses might be hard to accept, if they are acted upon they can improve your life and the lives of those around you.

To dream of amputation signifies that you feel threatened by enemies and are helpless to do anything about them. While such dreams caution vigilance against those who have the power to 'wound' us, they also imply that we have the ability within ourselves to control our own destinies and need to take back the responsibility for our future destiny.

Medical instruments each have their own symbolism. Scalpels warn the sleeper not to take risks with their health, stethoscopes forebode indiscretion, and thermometers *(right)* remind us of the responsibility we owe others – to stop putting off until tomorrow tasks we know should be done today.

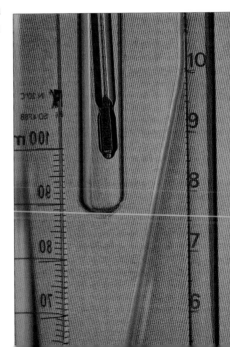

NEAR DEATH EXPERIENCES

The question of the existence of near death experiences is controversial, with neither side of the argument producing evidence that suggests an answer. While there are detractors who argue that such visions are more inner-body hallucinations than outer-body experiences, there are many men and women who have 'died' that are convinced otherwise.

An outer-body experience supposedly occurs when the soul leaves the body. This may be for several minutes or simply a fraction of a second. In nearly every case there are several common themes. The first is a feeling of leaving your body behind and travelling towards another place – often a radiant light at the end of a tunnel. The second is a return to your body as the patient is revived, often with an intense feeling of disappointment.

Such dreamlike experiences occur when the heart stops beating for a short time during trauma or major surgery. While this might seem frightening to some, most who have undergone a near death experience are left with a feeling of great inner comfort. All of us fear death and the prospect of an afterlife is comforting for many people. In dreamlore, similar visions of a

'life after death' are symbolic of new beginnings. Some people even suggest that at times of deep distress when the world seems impossible to cope with anymore, the brain will occasionally encourage the sleeper to dream of dying in order to cleanse their mind of their troubles and allow them to start anew. While this interpretation does appear somewhat simplistic, dreams that are similar to near death experiences certainly give the psyche extra clarity when it awakens, and a renewed ability and will to face and solve anxiety.

THE FINAL CURTAIN

"What dreams may come when we ourselves have shuffled off this mortal coil?" Most religions contain some concept of an afterlife. Whilst we cannot be certain what happens to us when the final curtain has descended, the image of death is invariably a melancholy bedfellow. The burial of a loved one is a naturally distressing dream, but ironically to envisage such an event in your sleep can be a positive experience. To see yourself attending a family funeral is, paradoxically, a sign that they are in good health and may soon be celebrating a happy event – often a wedding, an anniversary, or even a pregnancy. Meanwhile, to dream of your own funeral symbolizes that a particularly difficult phase will soon be over – you have buried the old, welcome the new!

Left: *To dream of an old-fashioned funeral procession with a large open glass hearse may demonstrate a wish to let others know the secret regard in which you hold yourself. This contrasts to the medieval approach to death, in which Man's mortality was actively espoused – as expressed in the fashion for cadaver tombs (below) where a 'warts-and-all' attitude prevailed.*

Coffins are complicated symbols in dreams; they also denote the transition from one stage of your life to another, via a range of emotions. While they may signal the end of an old relationship they also foretell of a new, happier one. Similarly they may signal that the dreamer will lose one job but gain a better one.

The most lasting symbol we leave behind is our grave. Dreams of neglected graves *(above)* imply that the sleeper has secrets they wish to conceal, while cracked or fallen tombstones warn that ambitions should never be held above personal contentment. Dreaming of your own grave can be traumatic and symbolizes problems in your waking life that you are literally trying to bury. One of the most widely reported nightmares is that of being buried alive. This is a particularly upsetting dream which usually occurs when the sleeper is under intense pressure in their daily life. The way to break free from such claustrophobic dreams is to examine your problems when awake and try to deal with each individually. For further help with breaking nightmares, see pages 244–247.

TO THE MEMORY OF
LIZABETH WILKINSO

EROTIC DREAMS

F reud believed that all dreams represented our deepest desires, which in adults were invariably wish fulfilment dreams about sexual activity. Today we appreciate that not all dreams are centred on sexual desire. Erotic dreams do not always simply represent our fantasies, but can reveal a lot more about our character. Those that regularly fantasize about pleasing themselves are often the kind of people that concentrate on self-gratification rather than the needs of others. Dreamers who imagine visiting 'ladies of the night' may, in waking life, be wary of personal commitment; and those who fantasize about promiscuous sex often harbour feelings of personal inadequacy.

Certain parts of the human body contain more sexual connotations than others – the breasts and penis being obvious examples – yet there are other, more subtle images that have come to represent our sexuality that we may not openly associate with sexual activity. One such example is the classic dream symbolism of the lock and the key, where the action of placing the key within the lock corresponds intimately to the roles of male and female.

SEDUCTIVE DESIRES

A ll stages of the seduction process, from first meeting to finally making love, are represented in our dreams, and each carries their own symbolism. Desire is an important emotion in a relationship and in dreams those we appear to lust after may seldom be the type of partner we would normally crave. In today's world where sexual imagery is used (and abused) by advertisers to encourage us to buy all manner of unlikely products, our brains absorb a range of erotic images that might be released in sleep. Thus, having erotic dreams is seldom unusual given the bombardment our minds receive – and should never be considered a damning reflection of personal proclivity.

In dreams, as in life, flirting can be a sign of your intentions or simply a harmless diversion. To dream of flirting with a friend or a colleague at work should not be taken to imply a desired outcome, but is more usually taken to suggest a desire for more excitement or challenges in your working life.

Kissing in a dream *(opposite page)* can be extremely sensual and often leaves us with more pleasant memories when we awake than if we imagined a fuller sexual scenario. Occasionally, however, kissing an inappropriate partner can also leave us feeling ashamed when we wake –such dreams underline taboos and boundaries that the psyche has set, and should not be crossed in waking life. To see yourself kissing someone that you really like is usually wish-fulfilment and should not be taken as a sign that they return your feelings; more fortuitous might be a dream kiss with a mysterious partner – this may well symbolize the start of an exciting new relationship.

Dreaming of undressing in front of a lover shows that you are comfortable in their presence and are ready to share your secrets with that person or to commit to them at a deeper emotional level. However, to be shy or furtive suggests you are not yet ready for commitment.

Dreams of having sex in unusual positions or places suggest that the sleeper longs for more excitement and passion, and should seek new ways to enliven romance in the waking world. Having an affair within the realms of sleep also suggests a desire for greater sexual liberation – although not necessarily with a fresh romance.

Left: *Dreams of an erotic nature can simply be a release of pent-up sexual desires. In this context the type of sex we engage in is not necessarily amorous but is convenient to help us let off steam.*

COMMON SEXUAL THEMES

O ver recent decades our society has become more sexually liberated, yet many sleepers still feel ashamed of erotic dreams. Such dreams are common and should not be considered perverse. Sometimes they are a portrayal of our darkest secrets, but more often they reveal how we view ourselves and those around us than they do our sexual desires.

Role play is a common theme in dreams of an erotic nature. Seeing a partner adopt a guise that holds specific sexual resonance for the sleeper can be a way of expressing one's deeper desires; however, it also tells us a lot about our own personality. The characteristics we fantasize about are

often those we look for in a partner or long for in ourselves. Nurses *(opposite page)* or doctors represent the compulsion of another domain over your body; policemen and women exert authority and discipline, whilst strippers or the burlesque are perceived to cover more traditional territory.

Some erotic dreams can be extremely explicit, others are mildly implicit. Phallic images played with suggestively – such as a chess piece *(top right)*, or tantalizing glimpses of breasts and buttocks, can all be considered as erotic as dreams of full sex. These subtler dreams may illustrate the sleeper's desire to hide true emotion.

Dream fantasies involving prostitutes or orgies represent a desire for sexual experimentation, but their omens are seldom encouraging – the deep well of past morality surrounding such behaviour – as exemplified in Hogarth's *Rake's Progress (middle right)* – suggests ruinous debauchery.

Dreaming of sex with a member of the same gender does not necessarily reveal homosexual tendencies. Often the people we choose to sleep with merely personify characteristics we find attractive or long for ourselves.

Bondage and flagellation *(bottom right)*, or dream fantasies of bondage, represent a desire to relinquish control. It is an especially common dream for people who have high-powered jobs and who secretly long to hand over control to someone else for a while. It is also a way of relieving ourselves of the personal guilt we may feel towards our fantasies, as we metaphorically become the pawn rather than the player.

MEASURING UP TO SEXUAL ANXIETY

While sex is one of our greatest pleasures, it can also become one of our greatest worries. Few topics evoke more unnecessary concern than sexual performance, and its scope for personal embarrassment — yet most of us will have worried about it at some point in our lives. Unsurprisingly, such concerns are not restricted to our waking lives but also permeate our dreams.

The most common form of sexual anxiety is a fear of inadequacy. For men this is usually the appearance or size of the penis, while for women it may be their breast size or body shape. Dreams of sexual inadequacy directly mirror the fears the sleeper has in their waking lives. Sometimes the dream may exaggerate the problem out of all proportion, making it seem far worse than it really is. This may be compounded by the dreamer imagining themselves exposed in public, or being laughed at by a partner; however, this apparent sign of sexual inadequacy is rarely sexually motivated and is far likelier to point to other areas in the sleeper's life they consider to be a failure — perhaps mounting financial debt or a reversal of career opportunity.

The guilt of supposed sexual impotency in men *(left)* is a dream expression that invariably reveals an inability to cope with the events of the dreamer's waking life. However, things are rarely as bad as they seem, and if the dreamer begins to tackle their problems in a methodical fashion, they will be surprised at how easily they can regain control of their life.

Voyeurs spy on other people's experiences *(right)* for their own sexual gratification. These dreams display unease with your own sexual performance and a need for sympathetic reassurance from your partner.

140

LOVE

....

In dreamlore, as in life, the road to true love is never simple. Dreaming of a romance does not automatically signify joy and happiness; instead the ecstasy and the agony of love is reflected in equal measure by our dreams.

Jung identified that everyone has male and female aspects to their psyche, which he termed the 'anima' and 'animus'. The combination of these two aspects forms our views of the opposite sex and consciously and subconsciously helps us select our ideal partner. The anima and animus are particularly resonant in our dreams. The animus – masculine aspect of the psyche – helps influence a woman's view of her ideal man, based upon the influence of men in her waking life, most notably her father, brothers and past lovers. Whilst for men, the anima – the feminine part of the psyche – helps evolve what constitutes his idea of the perfect woman.

Our dreams may not always portend future events, although they offer up opportunities for us to grasp. Dreams reveal our unconscious desires and secret passions which, if we listen to the messages they send, will give us valuable insight into our emotional lives.

TRUE LOVE

Dreaming of love may reveal secret passions or a longing for a fresh dimension to our lives. Even those already in a happy and caring relationship may dream of falling in love with someone new. This is seldom a sign that we are unhappy with our current partner, but that we are looking for an added element to our life – this might simply be the desire to learn a new language, or it could be a signal to travel to strange and exotic locations.

Dreams of a new romance rarely promise a physical relationship. To dream of meeting someone and developing a mutual attraction suggests the dreamer's growing confidence and sense of increased self-esteem. Whilst this may help the sleeper realize their potential, they should take care not to let their increased confidence override practical considerations – take care to progress at a slow but steady pace, and 'don't try to run before you can walk'.

An idolized view of love and romance, such as those remembered from youth or depicted in old films *(right)*, may imply a 'perfect' match, but forewarns that once the trials and tribulations of everyday life start to impinge upon the relationship it is unlikely to last. Ironically, far more auspicious are dreams in which the sleeper has to work hard to win over the one they love; this demonstrates the sleeper's willingness to commit the time and trouble needed in order to make the relationship work. It further implies that the partner is worth fighting for.

To dream of falling in love with someone that is unattainable

is a sign of future disappointment. Although they may appear tantalizingly close, their love will always be beyond your reach.

Dreams of first love *(below)* are particularly poignant because they may hold so many bitter-sweet memories. In dreamlore first love represents innocence and, as such, demonstrates a longing to return to a simpler time. However, they can also serve to remind us of the mistakes we made in our past, warning us not to let jealousy or complacency destroy our current relationship.

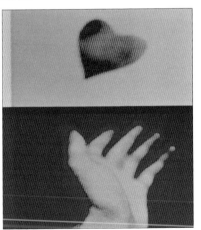

Above: When we fall in love we say that we have given our heart to someone. To dream of actually doing so should be taken as an encouraging sign of firm commitment.

COMMITMENT

Birth, marriage and death are the three milestones in our lives recognized by almost every religion and culture, yet marriage is the only one of these that we will consciously remember. Such a commitment is a massive step in any relationship and thus wedding imagery plays an important role in the symbolism of the dreamscape.

Even if you are in a committed relationship, to dream of becoming engaged should not necessarily be taken as a signal that your partner will soon propose; in fact it merely denotes that you are appreciated by another. This appreciation is usually a physical attraction, but can also symbolize gratitude for help you have given, or recognition of the role you have played in changing a life. Dreams of eloping are less fortuitous and imply disappointment in love or the failure of even the best laid plans.

Wedding dreams are often full of colour and vibrancy, directly reflecting the happiness of the married couple. To dream of attending a wedding is a

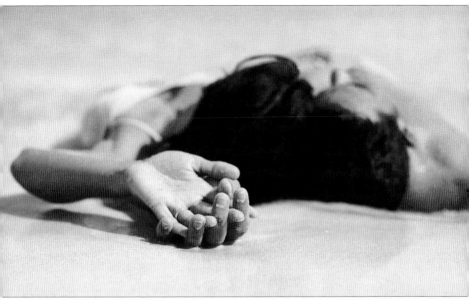

sign that plans will soon come to fruition. To dream of marrying someone you love (even if you or they are already married), is generally interpreted as the mind encouraging the sleeper to act more positively. If you are currently single the dream prospect of marriage symbolizes that two conflicting components of your life will merge to your advantage. However, to dream that you are reluctant to marry, or are forced to attend, may forewarn that your current partner may not be the right person for you.

In dream iconography, wedding rings *(opposite)* are an external sign of the internal commitment made between two people, and in dreamlore they represent faithfulness. To dream of someone placing a wedding ring on your finger is a sign that they care for you and will protect you in times of trouble. However, losing a ring can denote that you are becoming disillusioned with your partner. Dreams of being on honeymoon *(above)* herald the beginning of a much needed period of calm and stability in your life.

147

LOVE SOURED

A ll relationships will face periods of difficulty or strain, and many will unfortunately not survive. Dreaming of the breakdown of a relationship is not an omen that your partnership is doomed, but may reflect problems that exist in our waking lives that filter haphazardly into our dreamscape.

Dreaming that you and your partner are becoming increasingly alienated from each other and feeling as though you are constantly pulling in separate directions *(below)* is a sign that your relationship is under strain. While you may once have had shared ambitions, you feel as though you now have little in common. Given such prompts it is advisable to talk to your partner about what you both want out of life, and how to make your relationship stronger.

To dream of spying on a partner is a sign that you mistrust them. Whether or not this is likley to be merited, the sleeper should always avoid

cases the omens may be fortuitous, predicting a chance to start anew with one who will prove a far better match. Divorce may be harrowing in real life, but in dreamlore it signals independent actions and success through one's own efforts. Ironically it can also signify that the dreamer is in a strong and stable relationship.

Left: Dreaming that someone is spreading rumours about us, or those we love, may indicate that we secretly know something is wrong in our waking relationships.

letting jealousy and mistrust get the better of them. They may also like to examine their own conscious, as such dreams can be a sign of personal guilt mirrored back upon others.

To dream of being caught having an affair is a reflection of a personal folly or a guilty secret the sleeper may be harbouring in their waking life. Catching your partner in bed with another is often a sign, not that they are unfaithful, but that the sleeper's recent actions have been selfish and self-centred – if they do not change, they risk driving love away.

Dreams of being jilted by one we love *(right)* are often merely a sign of our own anxieties. However, in some

THOSE CLOSE TO US

O ur friends and family are the most important thing in our lives. They are our rock in times of trouble, our shoulder to cry on when things are going wrong and the people we look to to support us throughout our waking lives. Their importance to us means that their appearance in our dreams holds the power to be either comforting or distressing. While they may appear to symbolize security and support, dreams can warp events and personalities to leave us feeling lost and confused. To see those we love ill or endangered can be particularly uncomfortable – though this should never be seen as a portent of suffering, but merely our subconscious' way of reminding us how much they mean to us and never to take them for granted.

Without the waking boundaries of space and time, dreams can pervert people and events so that those we know may become unfamiliar. We may encounter our father as a young man, or our grandchildren as grandparents themselves. These images serve to remind us of our role in a greater picture, and that we are all part of a family that needs to love and support one another.

Dreams of THOSE CLOSE TO US

THE DREAMER'S FAMILY

Each individual member of our family occupies a unique place in our hearts and thus they retain this individual significance in our dreams. To dream of your parents demonstrates a longing for security or approval. Returning to the warm embrace of a loving mother or father *(left)* suggests

that we are finding it hard to cope with certain elements of our waking lives and seek the comfort that only our parents can provide. Mothers personify love and support, while fathers reflect a desire for authority or protection.

Sons and daughters reflect the pride we feel – not merely in our families, but also in our wider achievements. If the dreamer views themselves as a father with their son *(right)* it is important to observe the child's behaviour and emotions, as they reflect the dreamer's own individual strengths and weaknesses. The sleeper's aspirations may often be reflected in their child's actions. The relationship between mother and daughter *(opposite page, top left)* in dreamlore reflects the sleeper's emotional hopes or fears rather than their behavioural strengths or frailties.

Brothers and sisters are often the ones we turn to in troubled times, and to view one's sibling in a dream is an encouraging

sign of fortitude and the ability to overcome problems in the face of adversity. Even if you are an only child, to dream of having a brother or sister is a comforting omen, predicting a renewed sense of strength and energy in one's endeavours – the sibling may well be a personification of an idealized 'self'.

Grandparents, whether alive or dead, are synonymous with wisdom and knowledge. It is advisable to listen to any message they impart, especially for those who have unresolved issues in their waking lives. To dream of having a grandchild (real or imagined) is the personification of an inner sense of duty, a need to complete a set task – to see the 'wheel turn full circle'.

Right: *Some dreams involve happy images of our earliest memories. Although dreams will often change the small and incidental details, they still retain a sense of familiarity.*

BONDS OF FRIENDSHIP

Our friends are the family we choose, those with whom we can share our emotions and aspirations, joys and fears. In dreamlore, however, the role of these people – who often become closer to us than our own families – is varied and complex. Dreaming of meeting an old friend may simply be a nostalgic longing for a lost friendship, but it can also hint at a sense of loss in our current lives, or suggest a desire for moral support and guidance through a particularly difficult time.

The emotions expressed by a friend encountered in a dream are often more important than the people themselves. If they are happy and jovial it suggests the advent of a period of personal or romantic success; however, if they are worried or disturbed, the future may hold emotional upheaval.

Often in our dreams we are helped or supported by a 'friend' who we do not know in waking life. This may reflect a feeling that our current friends are not truly listening to us, although it is more likely the psyche's reminder to the sleeper that we owe a duty of care to those around us – not only those that we love and care for, but anyone who may be deemed to need our help.

Being betrayed by a friend may appear sinister, but it is not a sign that this action will be replicated in real life. More often it is an outward illustration of the insecurity we feel about losing those we love. Seeing a friend die in a dream is a

particularly distressing experience, although it should not be seen as an ill omen or thought to foreshadow a real event. Dreams such as these merely serve to remind us how much we should value our close friends – to fully appreciate them in the flowering of their friendship towards us.

Our neighbours can often become friends, but in dreamlore they assume negative omens. To be seen gossiping to a neighbour predicts rebounded trouble, whilst to meet them in a foreign city or an unfamiliar setting suggests a tedious task that must be acomplished, or an unwelcome guest whose presence has to be tolerated.

Above: Anxiety and fear for those we love can often creep into our dreams and lead us to believe that they are in danger. These dreams are expressions of concern, and never predictive.

VISIONARY FIGURES

To dream of someone you admire or look up to is understandable. Some of us seek to emulate the people we see in the media or read about in magazines and books. Dreams such as these can influence the type of person we aspire to be. Dreaming of someone famous does not mean that we necessarily long for fame, but is often a recognition that we wish to replicate their skill or an associated trait. They can prove a positive influence and inspire us to strive for our own success – although we should never become fixated with the triviality of lifestyle and the illusion of fame.

Teachers, policemen and judges are typically figures that may appear in our dreams when we need to seek the advice and guidance of those perceived to be in authority.

In our dreams we may adopt many different personae. They reveal the characteristics we may long to espouse – such as valour or reticence – yet they tell us more about the person we currently are, the wise man or the fool!

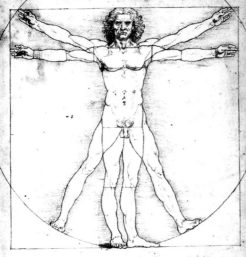

IMAGES OF SELF

Of all the people we meet in our dreams the strangest is often ourselves. We meet many people in our personal dreamscape, although they are often personifications of our own individual traits, emotions or aspirations.

The hero is a particularly popular image and one the dreamer may feel a strong affinity towards. They may take the form of a film star, action man or fictional warrior, each possessing a certain facet that the dreamer longs to emulate. Although they are often figures of wish fulfilment, sometimes heroes also reflect characteristics that the sleeper possesses of which they are currently unaware. Images of a mask *(left)*, or wearing a mask yourself, indicate that the dreamer is currently concealing, or wishes to hide, elements of themself. To be seen to remove the mask suggests that they are gaining in the confidence they need to truly be themselves.

Shadowy figures or unknown strangers may unsettle the sleeper and reveal elements of themselves that they find least appealing. The dream is often a reflection of our inner fears or unworthy desires that we know debase us. By confronting these figures in our dreams we can suppress the negative elements of our characters and guard against our own 'dark angels'.

Hermits, unsurprisingly, symbolize solitude, and suggest that the sleeper longs to have more time to themself. To be approached by a hermit suggests that the answer to one's problems lies internally rather than externally, and they should seek for wisdom inside, deep within themselves.

Finally, one of the most intriguing of all images of 'self' is that of the fool *(right)*. This talismanic image harks back many centuries to when the fool was valued not only for the amusement he provided but also for his wisdom – fools alone were allowed *carte blanche* to criticize a king surrounded by impotent sycophants – thus the only unbias and trustworthy advice came from the court jester. To encounter the fool is a sign that the dreamer has successfully balanced the two important elements of work and play.

Dreams of VISIONARY FIGURES

INSPIRATIONAL AND AUTHORITARIAN FIGURES

While dreams of meeting famous people can be seen as simple wish fulfilment, the appearance of the people we admire in our dreams also tells us something more about ourselves.

Often it is not the people that we meet in our dreams that are important, but the characteristics we associate with them. For instance, dreaming of Mother Teresa *(below)* may express a long held desire to help others less fortunate than yourself. Dreaming of meeting a current President or Prime Minister may represent a desire for success. Likewise, film stars and musicians imply a wish to emulate their skill and success. While some dismiss such dreams as idealist fantasy, they can benefit the sleeper. They may inspire you to take up an instrument yourself, to paint, dance or sing – whatever it takes to start you on the career path to eventually achieving your dreams.

While meeting a famous person in a dream can be inspirational, to

imagine that you regularly meet celebrities can have negative overtones. This is especially true if the sleeper sees themselves working for the celebrity. Such dreams hint at a feeling of inferiority and suggest that you feel overlooked or neglected in your waking life.

Figures of authority help shape our waking lives and their role in dreamlore is usually that of guidance and support. Outside the family, teachers have arguably the greatest influence on our childhood lives and consequently they are etched on our subconscious. The appearance of an old teacher in a dream is a sign

Dreams of VISIONARY FIGURES

that the dreamer requires structure in their life. They also warn us to seek the opinions of others we trust before making important decisions.

Policemen *(below)* traditionally symbolized protection and security, and the appearance of a uniformed officer in our dreams is an omen that help may arrive from an unexpected source. They also warn those with an important decision to make to choose the option they know to be right, rather than the one that feels easiest.

The appearance of a judge in a dream was once supposed to foretell the death of an enemy. However, their

Above: To dream of a past hero such as President John F. Kennedy is a sign that you admire them and wish to emulate certain characteristics associated with them, such as moral bravery and selflessness.

presence is now thought to signify the onset of a serious argument over a trivial matter. The blindfolded symbol of Justica, with her scales to weigh the evidence and sword to punish the guilty, is a more positive symbol, although the idea that she should wear a blindfold is a moot point, as justice should always be seen to be done.

FAITH AND WORSHIP

Dreams play an important role in many religions. Sections of the Qur'an were revealed to Mohammed in a dream; Jacob (the father of the twelve tribes of Israel) dreamed that he climbed a ladder to heaven and heard God promise him the land of Israel; while the Hindu text *Brahmavaiarta Purana* is a guide to interpreting the will of the gods through dreams. In every continent there are people who believe that their god can communicate through images received in sleep. Today, dreams are generally considered to be more closely linked to our psyche than to divine command, yet dreams of a religious nature still hold potency for believers.

Although God is never described in the Bible or Qur'an, dreams of God are surprisingly frequent. In the West he is often seen as a paternal figure with long white beard and flowing robes because this is the image traditionally given to children. If we dream that God has spoken to us – while this is unlikely to be a divine message – it may be something that our subconscious wants us to examine, and should be explored.

HEAVEN AND HELL

E ven for those who are not particularly religious, images of heaven and
hell hold specific symbolism. Heaven is associated with God, light and
goodness, whilst hell is linked to the dark menace of the Devil and evil.

Heaven is believed to be a place where the souls of those who have led a
good and virtuous life go when they die. It is usually thought to be located above
the earth and those worthy are 'raised up'. This image of uplifting is particularly

important in dreamlore. Dreaming
of heaven is a sign of elevation; this
may be a development of one's
spiritual beliefs, or in a temporal
sense can signify a promotion at
work or the improvement of one's
social situation.

Images of hell are far less
comforting. Deriving from 'hel',
the Teutonic word for 'to conceal',
hell is thought to be a place below
us where corrupt souls go to be
punished for eternity. Dreaming
of such a torturous place directly
reflects the state of the sleeper's
mind, highlighting troubles that
may be tormenting them. These
dreams often rely upon the
savagery of medieval imagery
to 'haunt' people who know they
have transgressed. Recurring
dreams of hell indicate that the
dreamer needs to rectify these
'sins' during their waking lives
in order to salve their conscience.

Above: *The Devil oversees a miser being
force-fed molten gold in Hell. His angelic
appearance as 'the Devil in all his feathers'
is a reminder that Lucifer is the fallen
angel... heaven and hell may be two sides
of the same coin!*

Dreams of FAITH AND WORSHIP

SYMBOLS OF FAITH

Churches, temples, synagogues and mosques are buildings of great spiritual importance; they hold an impressive sense of magnitude and reverence, even for non-believers. In dreams they are usually interpreted to represent our soul. Seeing an empty place of worship in a dream, devoid of furniture or decoration, is a sign that the sleeper has abandoned the beliefs they once held dear; whilst to envision a church or mosque elaborately decorated and thronged with worshippers suggests a re-awakening of the dreamer's own spirituality.

Images inside religious buildings are significant. The font in a church is a symbol of acceptance into the Christian faith, and represents ideas of renewal or redirection in dreamlore. The altar *(below)* is the focal point of the church, and to imagine one in a dream implies the discovery of inner peace. To stand with your back to an altar, however, forebodes approaching sorrows.

In Christianity bells are used to call people to church and in the realms of sleep they symbolize the arrival of good news. In Islam minarets are a sign of obedience and devotion and in dreams represent news of a spiritual nature.

Flowers (left) may be viewed decorating a church or temple, and their appearance in a religious context denotes a reawakening of the dreamer's inner spirituality. Other decorations, such as candles or statues, can enhance this new-found enlightenment, although they also hold their own distinct symbolism. A candle burning steadily represents consistency of belief. While statues embody intuitive awareness, telling the sleeper to listen to their instinct no matter what doubts they may experience along the way.

The cross was a sacred symbol long before the crucifixion. Celtic people wore it around their necks as a talisman to ward off evil spirits, but since the advent of Christianity it has become associated with the church. Dreaming of a cross tells the sleeper (whether they are a believer or not) that, although fate may have conspired against them, their period of ill luck will soon end. To dream of a holy book such as the Bible or the Qur'an indicates discretion and sensitivity – whilst to swear upon one tells the dreamer that despite criticism their current actions are correct.

Right: *Gargoyles were first used by the Celts to ward off evil spirits and were adopted by Christians as a way of protecting their churches. In dreamlore gargoyles tell the sleeper not to take people at face value; while this may warn about devils that appear fair, it also talks about angels that may appear foul.*

'HE WHO WOULD VALIANT BE'

Images of pilgrims *(right)* and martyrs represent those who have put their faith before worldly desires. Their role in dreamlore is to try and steer us towards the course of a 'better life'. Those that went on pilgrimage wished to demonstrate their faith to God and atone for past sins. For many, to envision undertaking a pilgrimage in a dream is a sign that the sleeper believes they have transgressed and need to atone for their 'sin'. For others it may be a sign that they wish to take time away from the hubbub of everyday life to discover their true self or to pursue a personal goal. If you are seen to go on dream pilgrimage, try to remember those that assisted you and the people who hindered your progression – they will have distinct character traits to be found in those we encounter in waking life.

Priests, rabbis and imams are all representative of people who have dedicated their lives to the service of their god. In dreams they may act as confidants, teachers or even parental figures – in each case the role that they assume is important. If the dreamer sees themselves talking to a pilgrim, it suggests that they have problems that can only be solved by outside intervention. To imagine themselves being taught by one suggests the dreamer is seeking guidance, whilst to be comforted is a sign they are reaching out for support in a venture or quest they feel unworthy to complete alone.

To dream of a saint – such as St George *(above)* – signifies spiritual protection and help in a noble venture. Martyrs have made the ultimate sacrifice, and if they appear in a dream it may be considered an omen that the sleeper will need to sacrifice certain elements of their temporal self to satisfy their spiritual integrity.

168

FABLES AND FANTASIES

··

Myths and magic have become increasingly less important in today's society. Whilst our ancestors would have believed in the existence of mythical creatures, such beasts are now relegated to the pages of children's stories. Despite this, their echoes still frequent our dreams, and often visions that we would regard as too fantastical for waking life find a place in the dreamscape.

Fairytales have become the last refuge of much of the magic that once coloured society, and much of its original symbolism has shifted. While dreaming of magic and enchantment may once have been seen to portend ill omens reflecting the ancient fears surrounding witchcraft, today such dreams hold far more positive connotations.

The spread of Christianity throughout Europe sought to undermine the pantheon of pagan creatures that were so popular before the arrival of the 'White Christ.' Churchmen played down the existence of these fantastical beasts in favour of their own brand of miraculous beings. Ironically, the angels *(inset)* and a host of heavenly messengers supplanted the old centaurs, giants and dragons, which are now regularly considered creatures of fantasy themselves.

HEAVENLY MESSENGERS

O ur dreams are a veritable treasure-house of symbolism, but sometimes when our subconscious wants one aspect to stand out above all others it evokes a particularly powerful emblem to carry that message. As the messengers of God, angels are an extremely vivid medium for this process.

If an angel *(right)* appears in your dream, it is advisable to take note of the message they impart. Angels may serve to steer you in the correct direction, warn you of potential danger, or reprimand you for past wrongs. Whatever

the case, the dreamer should take their advice seriously. Angels do not solely assume the role of messengers, and their presence in dreams may symbolize wisdom and protection. When the dreamer may feel upset or alone in the world, angels can act as guardians to the vulnerable – looking over them and empowering them with the energy needed to improve their situation.

Other emblems hold similar heavenly connotations. The symbolism of the Virgin originates long before the Madonna. She was known as Isis to the Egyptians, Myrrha to the Greeks and Juno to the Romans. The Virgin is commonly portrayed with a crescent moon at her head, although in dreamlore may also been seen with a lyre or flute *(above)* and a crown of stars. She is a favourable talisman that signifies a period of serenity is about to enter the dreamer's life.

The chalice *(right)* represents feminine values. The vessel is viewed as 'the well of the emotions'. If it is seen to be overflowing, the dreamer is likely to be ruled by the heart. The connection between the chalice and the grail can endow this dream symbol with a spiritual dimension.

Dreams of FABLES AND FANTASIES

MONSTROUS VISITATIONS

Our psyche is comprised of many conflicting components, and within the mind the darker elements that we consciously suppress in waking life are left to fester. In our dreams we may loosen the lease on these sinister factors and they become manifest in our dreams.

In the 4th century A.D. the christian philosopher Macrobius wrote a book entitled *The Commentary of the Dream of Scipio*, in which he argued that dreams were either controlled by God or the Devil and reflected the condition of the sleeper's soul. Today dreams of demons *(below)* may have lost their connotations of eternal

Right: *As with this illustration from a 1550s almanac, the monsters of our dreams tend to be ridiculous composites of our own worst imaginings. Upon careful reflection the creatures that stalk our nightmares can be revealed as the impostors they truly are.*

Dreams of FABLES AND FANTASIES

damnation, but they retain elements of a sense of moral corruption. To dream of a demon implies that the sleeper has a guilty secret that still haunts their subconscious. Any encounter with diabolical sources is generally interpreted to foreshadow a brush with temptation.

Gargoyles *(left)*, were placed on gothic churches and cathedrals in the belief that evil can be used to drive away other evil. Their presence in our dreams reflects this – and the more demonic and hideous they are seen to be, the greater is their power to protect. Gargoyles also indicate that we should guard against taking people at face value.

Werewolves *(below)* and vampires may manifest themselves in our dreams. They originate from medieval stories of the incubus and succubus, who were thought to drain the essence of their sleeping victims. These tales were added to by local legends and reports of the horrors perpetrated during the Crusades and Wars of Islamic Conquest. To dream of a vampire or werewolf warns the sleeper that someone, or something, is depleting the dreamer's spiritual force – perhaps a burden of worry that is 'draining them dry' of their psychic energy.

BALEFUL ENCHANTERS

In today's world there seems little room left for magic and mystery. Fairies, wizards and ogres are confined to children's books and no longer fill us with the literal sense of 'enchantment' that they once did. In our dreams, however, these mystic creatures still retain some degree of influence and should never be dismissed as childish images.

Fairies are now portrayed in children's books as benign creatures with butterfly wings that live in primrose and bluebell woods; however, the traditional view of them was somewhat different. Originally fairies were malevolent creatures that played tricks on mankind in order to hurt us. In dreamlore they retain much of this traditional imagery, warning us to beware those who appear to be assisting us, but who are in reality acting only for their own gain. Similarly, willow-the-wisps and other fire spirits *(below)* that used to lure travellers away from the safe paths through dangerous marshlands, also serve to warn us against those people that appear to be helping us, but who ultimately want to see us fail.

To encounter an ogre or giant in a dream is a sign that we will face problems in our waking lives. The larger or more fearsome the ogre, the harder the obstacle will be to overcome. Their presence in the dreamscape may also link the giant's size to larger-than-life personalities we may be wary of (for example,

parents seem enormous to small childen) and so reveal the dreamer's lack of self-confidence.

Throughout history witches have suffered through negative association. As supposed harbingers of evil, anyone suspected of being a witch was blamed for the misfortunes affecting society and punished accordingly. Thousands of innocent victims were killed upon the pretext of practising witchcraft, and it is little wonder that in dreamlore witches were deemed to denote misfortune. To dream of meeting a witch foretold

Above: In Arthurian legend the sorceress Morgan Le Fay reflects the paradoxical nature of witchcraft – reflected in her duel role as both healer and dark magician; Arthur's enemy in life, yet his guardian in death.
Right: A medieval treatise on witchcraft includes this woodcut showing a wizard being taken to a sabbat by a demonic cat.

calamity. Now stripped of many of their negative connotations, witches are currently seen to represent a more enlightened form of magic. In today's dreamscape they represent the sleeper's desire to embrace gnostic knowledge and a higher plane of consciousness.

SUPERNATURAL BEASTS

Dragons, unicorns and other beasts of mystery are often described as the 'creatures of our dreams.' so perhaps it is only fitting that they find such poignant meaning in dreamlore.

The unicorn *(right)* is a creature that combines male and female imagery. It was said that only a pure virgin could tame the beast and, although this appears at odds with the phallic symbolism of its horn, the unicorns represent the perfect union of the masculine and feminine. The appearance of this magical beast in your dream may indicate a close friendship with a member of the opposite sex, which will seem like the union of two souls.

Dragons *(opposite page)* are one of the most potent animals in dreamlore. They symbolize a primal energy, neither good nor bad, but one which upholds the natural world. Like the unicorn, dragons represent the union of opposites, in this case the four elemental forces: their serpentine wings signify the flow of water; their breath, fire; their wings the element of air, and the caverns in which they dwell, represents earth. Due to their power, dragons are emblematic of inner strength.

Griffins combine the attributes of an eagle – foresight and sense of purpose – with those of a lion's strength. In dreamlore they symbolize vigilance. The sphinx is emblematic of mystery and divinity, and acts as a warning against self-deception; whilst centaurs – who combine the intellect of man with the power of a horse – caution against hasty behaviour and snap judgements.

Above: *According to medieval bestiaries, the griffin drew the chariot of Nemesis, and acted as a guardian of treasure – hostile to any who would seek to steal it.*

LUCK, SIGNS AND SYMBOLS

Mankind has an innate desire to seek signs of good fortune wherever he looks. Throughout history he has applied mystical qualities to innate symbols – often based upon only the most spurious of links. In numerology the number seven is considered lucky because it represents a closeness to God: having created the world He rested on the seventh day; there are seven virtues and seven layers of heaven; seven was also the sacred number of the Greek god Apollo and the Babylonian goddess, Ishtar. Thirteen is regarded as unlucky because it was the number of people at the Last Supper before Christ's betrayal by Judas.

Simple objects have assumed talismanic powers because of our need to be reassured that the power of 'luck' can be tamed and utilized to our own advantage. The horseshoe, four-leaf clover *(inset)* and rabbit's foot all now symbolize good fortune and are regularly used in daily life to try and persuade 'Lady Luck' to smile upon us. Because of the role they now play in our subconscious, these 'lodestones to fortune' have been absorbed into the symbolism of dreamlore. However, they tell us more about ourselves than they do about soliciting good luck.

TALISMANIC OBJECTS

There are many objects that we link to luck in our waking lives. Although we subconsciously associate most of these with good fortune, in dreamscapes their presence can also have a deeper meaning. Although not directly a talismanic object, the hourglass *(right)* immediately evokes powerful symbolism. As an unrelenting measure of time it is often associated with our own mortality. Just as the gradual trickling of sand reminds us that time is fleeting, the appearance of an hourglass in our dreams reminds us not to put off until tomorrow that which can be done today.

Crossed fingers *(below)* are a sign of desire for good fortune. Throughout history fingers have been seen as potent examples of sexual symbolism. In

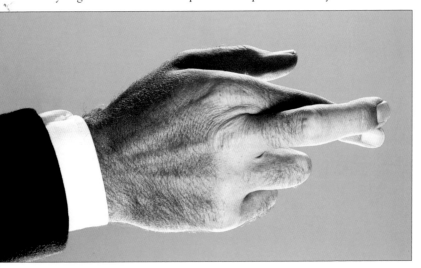

the Roman era it was believed that the middle finger was connected with the phallus, and in medieval society this finger was known as '*digitus infamus*' or 'the obscene finger', because it was the finger male prostitutes raised as a signal to potential customers. Even today raising the middle finger is seen as a lewd action. A crossed middle and second finger in a dream is sometimes regarded as a sign of sexual desire – the fingers mimicking the position of two lovers, one on top of the other.

If encountered in dreams, ladders are suggestive of an internal desire to strive for greater things. They demonstrate a desire for personal achievement, albeit in a professional or personal capacity. A fall from a ladder does not necessarily mean that you will be unsuccessful in your goals, but that you may need a greater

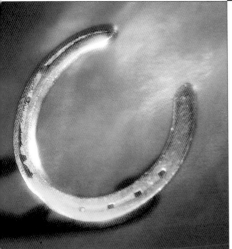

Above: *In Norse mythology as Thor, the god of thunder, rode across the sky he threw down his hammer to produce thunderbolts. In early dreamlore a vision of a hammer was said to provide protection against the bad luck of a lightning strike.*
Left: *A horseshoe is a traditional symbol of good luck and in a dreamscape foretells success in the face of pessimism.*

degree of self-belief, or a change of tactics to achieve your desires.

Wells and fountains are among the most magical symbols to imagine in your sleep. They are associated with healing and wish fulfilment. By dreaming that you throw a coin into a well or fountain, you continue a ritual that dates back thousands of years to when votive offerings were thrown into the water to appease the '*genus loci*' or local deity.

THE POWER OF NUMBERS

Numbers are a surprisingly common element in dreams, but it is rare for us to remember them when we awaken. Therefore, those numbers that we do recall are important, because each has a specific resonance within dreamlore. Here we will explore the numbers one to nine.

The number one is associated with the soul and denotes independence and individuality. The number two represents union and companionship and can signal the start of a new relationship or the cementing of an old.

Three is the most common number in sleep and represents creation, whilst four is the number of balance and stability. The number five signifies energy and is associated with a desire for adventure or freedom. Six is believed to be the number of harmony and equilibrium, stemming from the belief that the world was created in six days.

Seven is generally regarded as the luckiest number because it represents man's relationship with God, who instigated the seven virtues and seven sins.

Eight symbolizes old age and death, although in dreams it is seen as a beginning of new horizons rather than decay. Finally, nine symbolizes growth and pregnancy (after the nine months a baby spends in its mother's womb) and often foretells of a fresh development or a change of circumstance.

Left: Many believe that numbers in dreams are a premonition of what horse to back or what numbers to play on the lottery. Even a dream in which the sleeper gambles and wins is not a sign of wealth, but rather an innate desire to achieve this. Numbers in dreams represent emotions and energies, not signs of how to achieve personal wealth.

COLOUR IN YOUR DREAMS

Colours have the ability to arouse powerful emotions and in dreams are highly symbolic. The colour red represents excitement, anger, aggression and sexual energy. It stirs up desires in the dreamer to act now and to put their emotions before all else in order to achieve their desires. Dreams that are bathed in an orange glow are calmer and signify a sense of hospitality and openness that promises improvements in the sleeper's social life. Yellow, meanwhile, is an emotionally balanced colour – it helps release the dreamer's tension and may be accompanied by creative thoughts that the sleeper should try to act upon when they awake.

Blue is the colour of spiritual understanding. It radiates compassion and strength of mind. It is the antithesis of red and warns the dreamer to act upon clear thoughts rather than reckless emotions. Purple has similar connotations and is closely linked with meditation and inner forethought.

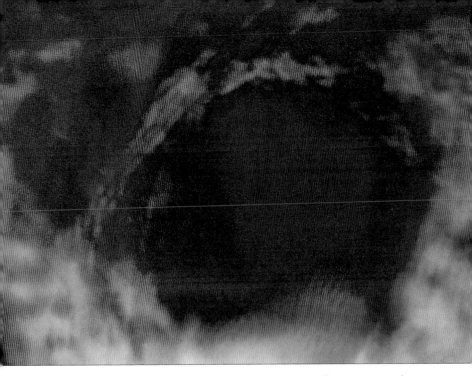

Green represents healing and growth and, if seen when ill, is an extremely positive omen of improved health. However, for those in love it is less positive, as it indicates jealousy and mistrust in either the dreamer's mind or that of their partner.

Our inner psyche closely associates black with death, but in dreams it more commonly represents entrapment or the fear of the unknown. Falling through darkness implies a fear that the dreamer has in waking life. This commonly includes a reluctance to become involved in a relationship, unsettled feelings involving a career change, or an unwillingness to espouse new ideas. However, black is the colour of intransigence and suggests that these worries may be based, not on the dreamer's fear of the issues themselves, but simply upon their dread of the unknown, and therefore should be conquered rather than embraced.

White opposes all aspects of black. It is the colour of innocence, purity and assurance. It suggests that the dreamer is currently making the right decisions in their life and that they should proceed as they believe appropriate, despite potential opposition. Emerging from black into white is an extremely encouraging omen and illustrates a dreamer's ability to break away from their fears, and to transform the negative aspects of nightmares to the sleeper's advantage.

FOOD FOR THOUGHT

Not only do we need food and drink to nourish and sustain us, it is also one of our greatest pleasures. Even when awake we sometimes daydream about the foods we love, thus it comes as no surprise that its images infiltrate our sleep.

Specific foods have their own dream symbolism, and even the preparation, presentation and way we eat our food all invite interpretation. To dream of hosting a dinner party implies harmony and friendship, whilst picnics foretell guilty pleasures and surreptitious enjoyment.

The type of meal we see ourselves eating can also play a role. Breakfasts talk of a wealth of opportunity that lies invitingly in the dreamer's path; a rushed lunch may imply impatience, and dinner is a meal of many shades. To eat alone forecasts a re-assessing of priorities, those that share a meal are likely to forge lasting friendship, while those who argue at table may find that stubborn or unworthy acts will alienate those who they hold most dear.

Generally, the symbolism of food is considered to be fortuitous; however, if we over indulge, the omens associated with food will quickly be reversed.

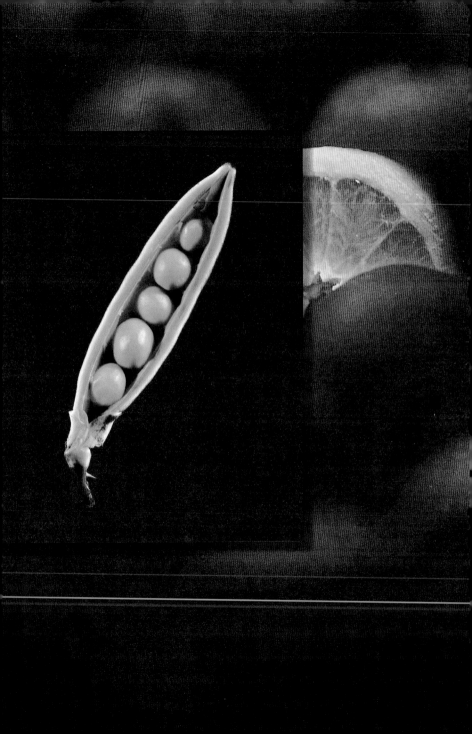

BASIC INGREDIENTS

While food can be one of our greatest pleasures, we should not forget that we eat to live, rather than live to eat. Just as the foods we enjoy have their own individual significance in dreamlore, so too do the basic foods that form the basis of our daily diets *(below)*. Salt and pepper *(above)* add interest to our pallet yet neither denotes fortuitous omens. Salt is seen to represent youthful exuberance and inflamed passion, whilst pepper signifies rumour and intrigue.

Dreams of any form of abundant harvest – especially corn – are suggestive of reaping the rewards of hard work. However, if the sleeper envisions a bare field or a diseased plant, this is an indication that their luck will soon change for the worst and that they need to make preparations now for harder times to come. Bread represents peace and wellbeing. Kneading dough in a dream shows a confidence in our own abilities, whilst breaking bread with others demonstrates the value the dreamer places upon the bonds of friendship.

Dreams of Food and Drink

Our taste in food stems from our childhood likes and dislikes *(left)*. As we progress through life we become more willing to try new and more exotic recipes. Dreaming of eating food that we may never have tried in our waking lives is a sign that the sleeper is willing to open their mind to new experiences and is willing to espouse alternative or even radical ideas. To imagine eating food you know you dislike demonstrates a desire to please others at a personal cost to yourself.

In dreamlore potatoes (below) have come to represent stability in the home, and earthy responses to earthy problems. To see yourself eating this food staple implies reticence, but with a decided lack of imaginative flair. To dream of harvesting the crop is emblematic of hard work – if the yield is worthy of your efforts, then you should be successful in a future enterprise; however a blighted crop forewarns of problems ahead.

The omens relating to meat are far from propitious, and generally it is considered to represent lust and pent-up emotion – highlighting the 'sins of the flesh', in which a loveless sexual encounter may be likened to two dead carcasses joined but devoid of the living soul.

Rice is another staple food of many diets and denotes confidence in business ventures, stemming from one's power to grasp and master innovative ideas and inventive propositions.

GREEN CUISINE

Dreaming of planting vegetables is a sign of a need for future planning, suggesting that the dreamer should start concentrating on the future rather than the present. Those that see themselves picking vegetables will soon be rewarded. However, if the vegetables harvested are mouldy or rotten, this is a sign that the sleeper's plans are doomed to fail.

Each vegetable, and even their condition, has dreamlore significance. Wilted cabbages denote disappointment in love, rotten cauliflowers signal failure due to a neglect of duty, and mouldy onions speak of spite and envy. Carrots are more encouraging, portending happiness and health – in women they may forecast pregnancy or the promise of a large family. However to see a carrot dangled tantalizingly in front of you but just out of reach *(left)* uses trite symbolism to suggest that your dreams are currently beyond your grasp, but through hard work you should eventually attain them.

Asparagus *(below)* if picked in a dream implies obedience and if eaten can denote success. In its capacity as an aphrodisiac asparagus promises the dreamer exciting sexual encounters – though if the plant has a bitter taste they are warned that the relationship will end in tears.

Cutting onions *(right)* denotes sadness and emotional pain. Just as the action of peeling onions or chopping them may make your eyes water, dreams may use this imagery to caution the sleeper that selfish or inappropriate actions may have made others cry. Dreaming of eating a raw onion may signify a flaw in your personality, whereby your obstinate insensitivity is known to everyone but you!

While debate surrounds whether a tomato is a vegetable or a fruit, its role in dreamlore is clearer. Picking a tomato forebodes bad luck and libellous gossip, though eating it indicates the recovery of lost esteem. Beans and peas *(below)* indicate that the dreamer has an important decision to make in their waking lives – the choice of action, however, will become complicated, as all options will appear to be of equal merit.

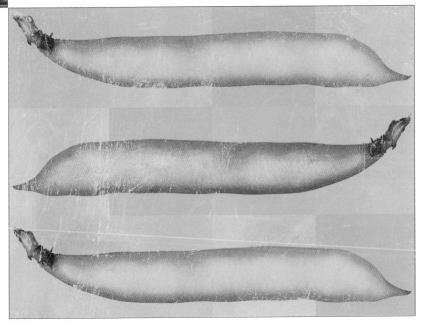

FORBIDDEN FRUIT

Fruit holds a wealth of sexual symbolism, dating back to the biblical account of Adam and Eve biting into the forbidden fruit in the Garden of Eden and noticing their nakedness. Over time, many and various fruits have developed increasingly erotic connotations which are relevant within dreamlore.

Cherries *(right)* are a voluptuous fruit, which in shape resembles the buttocks, breasts or even the lips. They hint at a future sexual encounter, but the joy we get from this depends upon whether the cherries are thought to taste bitter or sweet in our dreams.

To see yourself eating a peach *(right)* is regarded as forecasting good fortune. In China peaches are considered particularly auspicious, as they are associated with the god of long life, Shou-hsing, who is frequently depicted holding a peach plucked from the gardens of Paradise.

Thanks to Eve's gift to Adam, apples *(below)* are linked to original sin – considered by the early Church to be represented by the act of lovemaking. In the Middle Ages there was such stigma surrounding sex that the Church even produced manuals of how and when intercourse could morally take

place. Instruction forbade sex on a Sunday and during religious holidays; it should never be for pleasure but simply to procreate. Today we have evolved a more relaxed attitude towards sex, but in dreamlore apples still carry their earlier caution against letting ourselves be ruled by our libido.

Oranges speak of short but sweet encounters, grapes of a long and affectionate union, and strawberries of true love. Lemons however, represent bitterness and jealousy; whilst blackberries and raspberries indicate emotional entanglements and infidelity.

Dreams of FOOD AND DRINK

NAUGHTY... BUT NICE!

" I can resist everything except temptation."While we know that we should only eat the foods that are bad for us in sensible moderation, today's consumer-based society where treats are easily available makes temptation hard to refuse. Foods that we enjoy can hold auspicious omens in dreamlore but just as in waking life too much of a good thing can be bad for us.

Whilst dreaming of treating yourself to an occasional bar of chocolate or a cream cake indicates reward for effort, over indulging or bingeing on treats will negate any positive meaning. To dream that you over eat until you are sick is a sure sign that the sleeper has become too greedy for their own good, but also that they stand to lose everything they have worked for unless they change their ways. To dream of hoarding food is a sign of selfish intent and warns the sleeper to share with others or risk losing all that they have.

Despite the general connotations our favourite foods hold, they also have their own individual symbolism within the dreamscape. Cakes are representational of 'giving'. To dream of being handed a piece of cake by another is a sign that you are held in high regard by colleagues and friends. To see oneself sharing a cake with others is indicative of a generous personality and demonstrates the sleeper's tendency not to limit their friendship to one person, or a group of people, but to bestow their affections on a wide social circle. Linked to this, pastries denote heartfelt friendships, and biscuits indicate a warm and generous persona.

Childhood favourites like ice cream *(left)* tend to reawaken the 'inner child' within us all – such dream topics should be enjoyed as they presage success in ventures already underway. To dream of children eating ice cream denotes security and loving happiness within the home, but if it is seen to melt this implies a wish that will remain unfulfilled. Dreaming of eating jelly *(below)* or old-fashioned sweets *(opposite page)* are likely to predict a reunion with a childhood friend – or even a sweetheart.

Above: *Chocolate is believed to represent a desire to make money. Those that dream of eating chocolate enjoy spending their earnings, while those that hoard their treats have a more considered approach to the future – although they should beware of developing miserly tendencies.*

EXCESS!

A classic dream of ill fortune is the omen
of mice or rats eating your food *(right)*
– anciently said to forecast starvation. While such
dreams of poverty do not bode well, to be seen to
eat to excess in a dream can hold similar portents
of bad luck. Consuming too much of something we like can negate its positive
meaning *(see pages 196–7)* and in dreamlore any form of overindulgence will
be viewed by the psyche as dangerous backsliding.

   To dream of attending a bountiful banquet overflowing with lavish foods
and drink and surrounded by other guests may seem wonderful to some,
yet while the sleeper may concentrate on the luxurious food, it is the rest
of the dreamscape that is significant. The food merely distracts the dreamer

from the fact that they are
seldom spoken to by any of
the guests at the banquet and
they rarely eat anything. Such
dreams, in which the sleeper
merely becomes part of the
background rather than a
protagonist in the scene, are
considered ominous. Here
the banquet may represent

*Left: To dream of a jovial fat man
carving a joint of meat may appear
a happy vision but in fact signals
poverty, vexation and ill temper.
The man symbolizes gluttony and
greed while the meat denotes your
own life-force that he is cutting
into for his own gain.*

health and friendship, and because the dreamer feels excluded the dream's symbolism may suggest illness or social exclusion.

Eating too much represents a lack of self control. Dreams in which we eat until we are sick, or in some exaggerated cases until we 'burst', indicate the sleeper needs to curb their baser desires before they lead them into trouble. Dreaming that you continually eat but never feel full is a sign that the dreamer is failing to find rewards in their life – it suggests they may need to think about changing to a more rewarding job, or undertaking some form of charity work in order to make a tangible difference to their world and that of others around them.

Sometimes in dreams we are hurt by the foods we crave. We may see ourselves literally 'slipping on a banana skin' *(above left)* or eating something that we know to be poisonous *(above right)* – but that we eat anyway! These dreams reflect the danger of eating too much in real life; telling us that although we feel comforted by some foods, they are actually causing us far more harm than good.

'DOWN THE HATCH'

Dreams of alcoholic drinks can be double-edged. While seeing oneself enjoying a drink with friends can be a fortuitous sign of social 'lubrication', intoxication invariably forbodes disgrace and personal shame.

Seeing others who are drunk in dreams can be ominous. Just as Noah's son Canaan was punished by God for seeing his father intoxicated, the dreamer could suffer similar repercussions by losing respect for those they had previously held in high regard. To see the devastating and debilitating affects that drink can have on people's lives – as in Hogarth's rumbustiously moral etching 'Gin Lane' *(above)* – could be your subconcious mind imploring you to help someone that you suspect might have a problem with alcohol.

To dream of drinking wine or champagne *(opposite)* indicates a need for discretion to avoid public criticism. Beer can denote disappointment, and cider cautions that you may have been squandering money on material possessions which could have been put to better use.

As a general rule, a dream's portent is dictated by the nature of the drink – is it wholesome and thirst quenching, or is it used for intoxication? Fresh or clear water *(left)* symbolizes health and a cleansing of body and spirit. To imagine drinking warm water in a dream signifies sickness. Unsurprisingly, to dream that you swallow stagnant water or sea water forbodes the embarrassment of violent sickness.

LEISURE PURSUITS

··

Nowhere in dreamlore are the two conflicting
emotions of ecstasy and agony better represented
than in sport. Dreaming of winning can raise our spirits
and make us feel proud of ourselves, yet being beaten
to a prize that remains tantalizingly illusive can upset us
and leave us in a bad mood even after we wake. While
athletic prowess in a dream can be linked to feelings of
emotional wellbeing, it is not a simple case of winning
portends 'good luck' and losing 'bad'. As with life, in the
dreamscape, the taking part is often more important than
winning and often it is the sport or leisure activity we are
involved in that is more symbolic than the outcome.

While individual sports and leisure pursuits each
contain their own symbolism, if we regularly dream about
taking part in any sporting activities or expressing our
artistic skills, we are being encouraged to make changes
to our lives. This could simply mean becoming more
physically active, or making the most of the talents we
are lucky enough to possess; or it may be that we need to
re-assess the way we spend our waking lives and set aside
more time for the activities that make us happy.

WHAT PRICE VICTORY?

I n the dreamscape images of winning are highly emotive and can fill us with an enormous amount of pride and self-satisfaction, yet in our dreams, as in real life, it is not the victory that is truly important but the manner in which it is achieved.

To visualize winning a hard fought contest can feel personally satisfying. By employing dreams such as these our subconscious mind is able to depict the bravery and dedication we need to display in our waking lives –to find a 'cause' worthy of our time and effort. For others dreaming of a hard-earned 'victory against the odds' could imply that the sleeper has abilities that have previously been suppressed but may, if they believe strongly enough in themselves, be released to help achieve goals once considered impossible.

Dreaming of competing in sports such as tennis *(opposite)*, squash or badminton, in which you compete against an equal, is a sign that you are

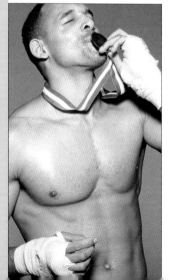

undecided about a choice you will shortly have to make in waking life. If you imagine winning trophies or medals *(left)* this suggests you will make the correct decision; however, if you lose or bend the rules to achieve victory this implies that you need to be careful of taking a snap decision which may lead to disaster.

Cheating in a dream is a sign of self-deceit: despite what you might be telling yourself about the 'greater good' or 'what they don't know won't hurt them', you know deep down that your behaviour is wrong and that you need to be more honest with yourself as well as other people.

Dreams of LEISURE PURSUITS

Dreams of LEISURE PURSUITS

SPORTING METAPHORS

From the gladiatorial games of the Roman Coliseum to the jousts of medieval knights *(right)*, mankind has been fascinated by watching protaganists battle for supremacy. From these early 'life or death' contests has developed the sporting challenge, and given dreamlore the metaphor of two equals struggling for supremacy.

The most obvious link to the bloody duels of the past is boxing *(below)*. Here two people still use their skill and endurance to fight for ascendancy. Boxing's link to individual combat ensures that in dreams it has come to represent an internal battle fought within the sleeper – where two conflicting issues remain unresolved. To dream of participating in a fight may represent a clash between the dreamer's public and private persona. Watching a boxing match indicates that the dreamer will enter a period of uncertainty in their life in which they will struggle to know right from wrong. Although this unbalanced period will eventually pass, they should be sure to listen to their head rather than their heart.

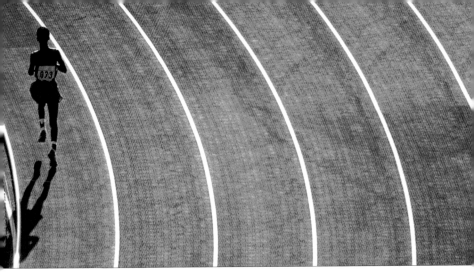

Although less violent, other sports still represent this antagonistic clash of wills. Athletics events represent man's fight against themselves as well as each other, as they continually strive to push their bodies to the limits of endurance. Dreaming of running in a race *(above)* encourages aspiration – to be top of your profession, where other competitors represent obstacles you will need to overcome in the 'race' to achieving success.

Watersports, such as sailing or swimming, combine the element of competition with the symbolic purity of water. These dreams speak of a desire to achieve a goal, not for the dreamer themselves, but for the good of others.

Fencing *(right)* is another sport that harks back to the idea of hand-to-hand contest, and in the dreamscape signifies a clash of morality. These dreams may occur when the sleeper is emotionally entangled with an unsuitable partner, or when they are doing something for themselves which they know will hurt others.

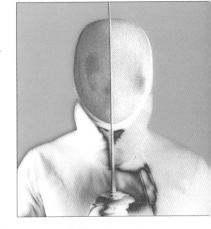

Dreams in which the opponents rely upon their superior skill to claim victory, represent the dreamer's desire for greater independence. Similarly, to imagine participating in a gymnastic event also speaks of the sleeper's desires for a greater degree of freedom and self-expression.

GET ACTIVE!

W e all know that we need to exercise to keep our body healthy, but this remains a message many ignore. Dreaming of exercise is our psyche's less-than-subtle way of telling us we need to 'get active' – for our own good.

Dreaming of taking part in a vigorous activity that we have never done before is an invitation from the subconscious to extend our horizons – both in terms of exercising the body and 'living life'. It may be that we have let our fitness levels slip and our psyche is telling us to 'pick up the pace', or that we have settled into a daily routine which is limiting our opportunities in life. In today's hectic society where we seem to be constantly busy, dreams of change usually represent a need to re-assess priorities and make time for things other than work. Dreaming of new activities is a poignant way of telling us we need to make more time to spend on our health and personal fitness.

To dream of running *(below)* may be either liberating or excruciatingly painful. Jogging represents the dreamer's desire to achieve a personal

Left: Running with one you love denotes sharing an ambition with a partner. This may be starting a family, saving to buy a house or planning a wedding. It also suggests that you are both eager to strengthen your relationship and drive it forward.

Above: Dreaming of challenging exercise in which we may be caked in mud and sweat, represents the dreamer's willingness to push themself to the limits in order to achieve a personal goal — to strive forward with but one ambition, despite distraction and pain!

ambition. To dream of being able to run at fantastic speeds, or leap incredible distances and never tire indicates that the sleeper should achieve the success they desire easily. However, to struggle slowly over rough terrain, with sore feet and aching legs, is a sign that achieving your desires will involve a much greater effort than you realized. To dream of struggling on despite the pain and hardship is indicative that your determination will eventually prevail.

Any dreams of exercise are seen as a gentle reproach to start on the path to a more healthy life. If you have done little exercise in the past, discuss feasible targets with a health professional before committing yourself to a fitness regime.

HIGHS AND LOWS

In dreams swimming *(right)* is a sensation closely akin to unaided flight. The feeling of water passing over the body led Freud to link dreams of swimming with sexual intercourse. Swimming represents a freedom from social constraint and is the mind's way of releasing tension through dreams. Drowning, however, suggests that the sleeper feels overwhelmed by problems in their life and is finding it hard to cope with the pressures placed upon them. In persistent cases of 'drowning' it may be advisable for the dreamer to seek the help of a trusted friend in whom they can confide to help them unburden their worries.

To see oneself climbing in a dream is a sign of personal ambition. The climb is symbolic of the dreamer striving to 'reach higher'— the tougher the ascent, the greater will be the reward. Visions of falling are one of the most disturbing, yet frequently reported, themes. Although vertigo or falling may presage a shattering of the dreamer's ambitions, this sensation of slipping

through the air into nothingness is more closely associated with stress, fear and anxiety in waking life. During such dreams the sleeper will often jolt awake with a sense of horror at the fall. In such cases it is important to stay calm and try to remember what it was that caused the fall, as this will hold a clue to what is most troubling you.

Left: While dreams of climbing represent the dreamer's desire to achieve their personal goals, to see oneself slipping or falling will be a sign that you have set these aspirations too high and that you need to re-assess your ambitions.

'HIGH ROLLING'

To dream of gambling and winning can seem like an auspicious omen – forecasting luck and the tantalizing prospect of future wealth. However, these visions are a mere reflection of the dreamer's desire for 'easy money', and if acted upon are more likely to lead to failure than success and prosperity.

Dreams are greatly influenced by daily life, and if we spend time reading the names and numbers of horses or thinking of lottery numbers, our subconscious mind will absorb this overload of information. In sleep our brain reviews and releases data and ideas that might be considered 'surplus to

Above: *Although we may dream of a certain horse winning a race, or believe we see a number or name emerge in our sleep, the images we envision represent a desired outcome of wishful thinking – and seldom, if ever, the correct forecast to a sporting event.*

requirement'. Most we forget by the morning, but occasionally we may half-remember an unusual or distinctive name (perhaps one with resonance to our waking life) which is then wrongly assumed to be a prediction inspired by supernatural intuition. Our dreams cannot foretell the results of a race or predict lottery numbers. Once in a while a 'hunch' might prove successful – but statistically you would be just as successful if you randomly stuck a pin in a page from the racing papers pointed at a series of muddled numbers!

Dreams of gambling exert strong omens in dreamlore, and display moralistic simplicity in their symbolism. It is widely believed that the fortune the sleeper experiences whilst gambling in their dream will be reversed in real life. According to an old American almanac, to see oneself winning a game of dice *(top right)* foretells that the dreamer will 'suffer losses far greater than they and their family can afford'. While to win at cards *(middle right)* fulfils the old proverb 'lucky at cards, unlucky in love'. However, if the sleeper is seen to lose, the omens are reversed.

Although playing chess *(bottom right)* seldom involves chance, as a dream omen it is utilized by the psyche to express analytical thought, yet carries implications of smugness.

MUSIC IN OUR DREAMS

M usic is usually a positive omen in our dreams. To hear music in
sleep indicates a sense of harmony in your waking life, suggesting
equilibrium between social relationships, family concerns and your career.
However, on rare occasions when the music is out of tune it warns of social
friction, whilst sad or discordant music forbodes hurt and upset.

Microphones *(below)* amplify sound, and if the sleeper imagines them
being used in a dream the meaning of that dream is likewise amplified. If you
hear yourself singing in a dream, it is important to take note of the type of
song you sing. Hymns denote contentment, sea shanties a thirst for adventure,
operatic melodies a desire to express oneself succinctly, while songs we
remember from our youth imply a desire for a less complicated lifestyle.

Musical instruments hold their own symbolism, and to dream of playing one
(even if in waking life you would not know one end of that instrument from the

other) suggests that you actually please a loving partner – even though you sometimes doubt it. To imagine playing the piano signifies that you will find a valuable object in the most unlikely place. Guitars *(above left)* suggest a nimbleness and lightness of touch when dealing with difficult situations. Saxophones *(above right)* and other brass instruments hold out the prospect that something unexpectedly interesting will shortly happen. Drums, which are seen to mimic the rhythm of the heart, predict love, but with complications attached. To the ancient Celts harps represented the passage of the seasons, and to hear their strings in dreams is a sign that the sleeper needs to be more 'in tune' with nature.

Right: Trumpets may suggest that the dreamer is becoming too boastful. Here the phrase 'don't blow your own trumpet' is particularly poignant – warning the dreamer to curb their conceit before it alienates others.

THE ARTS

In dreamlore, as in real life, the arts can bring great pleasure. Their appearance in our dreams can inspire greatness in us all – to remind us of hidden talents, or give expression to muted aspiration.

Dreaming of undertaking an artistic pursuit demonstrates the sleeper's subconscious desire to explore their own gifts. It encourages them to make more use of the talents they are aware of and pursue different fields and genres in which to develop them.

As discussed previously, music is symbolic of harmony, and if the dreamer sees themselves conducting an orchestra *(above)* it implies that they hold the wellbeing of others in their hands. In some this can demonstrate a desire to manipulate others, but for most people it is an external sign of the internal sense of responsibility they feel towards a family member or a loved one.

If the dreamer visualizes themselves watching an opera, it is important to remember the type of performance they attend, albeit comedy, drama or tragedy – each will loosely mirror future prospects in the dreamer's life.

Dancing expresses the sleeper's inner feelings of joy, reflecting their current lives and their future prospects. However, if they see themselves tripping or falling, this may be taken as a sign that they will suffer a setback, whilst to dream of watching the ballet suggests personal ambiguity.

Dreams in which the sleeper imagines themself an actor or actress may demonstrate that they have a difficult decision to make which has long-term repercussions – the audience's reaction to their performance is important.

Dreams of LEISURE PURSUITS

If the dreamer is applauded it suggests that their decision will meet with widespread approval, whilst if they are booed or are met with silence, the omens are far from perfect!

To visualize yourself learning lines for a production is suggestive of a need to seek the approval of your peers – to be seen to be 'going in the right direction' and 'making the right noises' in life generally.

To dream of reading *(above right)* indicates a desire to improve wider horizons, and it is important that the sleeper take note of the details of the book, as this will suggest possible routes to follow. Alternatively,the book you read may be your own – the psyche's prompting you to use your imagination to the full and produce that manuscript you have hitherto only 'dreamed about'. Likewise, dreaming of an art gallery *(below)* may be the subconscious encouraging the dreamer to discover the artist they know to lie within.

THE WORLD OF WORK

For most people, work fills a considerable percentage of our waking lives, and while we may hope to escape our jobs while we are asleep, dreams of our workplaces are common night-time visitations. The importance of our careers on our waking lives is mirrored in the dreamscape, where stresses and strains, fears and anxieties all reveal themselves to disclose the true state of our emotions. It is common for teachers to dream that they cannot control a class, for builders to see their constructions collapse or for brokers to lose millions on one wrong decision. However, none of these dreams should be taken as portents of the future or as a sign of personal incompetence – they are merely an external projection of our internal fears and the stresses we endure every day.

Due to the time spent at work, many of the objects we see and the people we meet will also find their way into our realm of dreams. Computers, desks – even the coffee machine – may all appear in our night-time visions. Some of these are important in their own right and possess their own individual meaning, whilst others merely serve to colour our dreams and familiarize the dreamscape.

WORKING 'ANGST'

The pressure of work gets to us all at some point in our lives, and although we might try to hide it externally from others, internally we cannot escape the stresses and strains which end up colouring our dreams.

Dreams of being under pressure reveal the very real stresses we face at the workplace. Although our dreams may exaggerate these worries or alter them significantly, the feelings that we are left with are all too familiar.

A common theme may involve visualizing a moving cog *(below left)*. This literally originates from the idea that we are all cogs in one giant wheel – our business! Such dreams might be particularly pertinent for those in positions of power – symbolizing the 'angst' they feel about their own position, and reminding them that they are just another component of one large machine.

Dreaming of having too much to do and too little time in which to do it *(below right)* is a sign that you are struggling to organize your time properly.

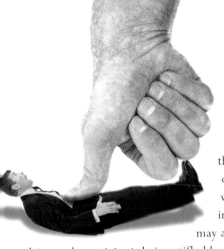

In such cases it is advisable to spend a little time planning your schedule. Dreaming of being under the thumb *(left)* is often a role reversal dream suffered by those in authority who fear losing their power and influence. Such dreams of suppression may also represent the feeling that our drive and creativity is being stifled by the selfishness and jealousy of others.

Fear of losing your job *(below left)* symbolizes how important your career is to you, but ironically augurs well for the future, hinting at success and possible promotion. Other work-related 'angst' may present itself in the symbolism of being late for the office *(below right)* which plays upon the dreamer's insecurities regarding punctuality.

WORKPLACE SYMBOLISM

Many spend so long at work that it is only natural that some of the images they absorb during the day find their way into their dreams. However, these objects are often more than mere reflections of our daily lives and each possess their own unique symbolism. In dreamlore the office rarely represents business matters. Usually they are more closely linked to the sleeper's personal and romantic life than to the sleeper's career. Dreaming of working in an office (even if you do not normally do so in your daily life) indicates that you have been neglecting one you love, and need to show them more warmth and affection. Visualizing yourself in someone else's office, with or without their permission to be there, suggests strong bonds of affection towards that person. However, for the sleeper to visualize themselves relocating to a new workplace could indicate a split with an old friend or the breakdown of a current relationship.

In a dream, the unconscious mind utilizes any object from which it feels able to derive symbolism. Thus items inside an office or studio each invite interpretation. An untidy office desk covered in papers indicates hurried

decisions that may cost the dreamer dear. Computers *(left)* have come to symbolize logic and order, and an inability to use them in a dream signifies that the sleeper may feel uncomfortable with technology, or that a particular project seems overwhelming.

Dreaming of attending a 'make-or-break' meeting *(above)* suggests that the sleeper has an important decision to make in their waking life – the outcome of which may affect many more people than just themselves.

There are many metaphors associated with the workplace, but one that infiltrates our dreams more than most is the idea of climbing the career ladder *(right)*. To see ourselves climbing to the top in a dream is a sign that we are striving to achieve our personal ambitions, whether they be in business or other areas of our lives.

MONEY MATTERS!

Money makes the world go round – and on a global scale it is what drives business and orders society, whilst on a personal scale it is the reason most of us get out of bed in the morning. We all need money to feed and clothe ourselves and our families, yet ironically in our dreams it represents the things no amount of wealth can buy – health, friendship and time to spend with those we care about.

To dream of being short of money denotes the sleeper's fears of illness and death, or negative feelings associated with self-worth. Finding money is a surprisingly common dream that promises future good fortune

– however this largesse must be spent wisely or the omens are reversed and the lucky dream recipient will fail to make the most of the opportunities granted to them.

Coins are considered to be fortunate talismen. To dream of having a bag or pocket full of coins speaks of rapid advancement along a chosen career path. To see yourself being handed a gold or silver coin indicates the fulfilment of an ambition or the beginning of a new relationship; while to possess a bronze or copper coin is a sign of achievement through hard work and the sweat of your brow.

To dream of investing your money wisely suggests a methodical (some might say 'plodding') mind, whereas to imagine hoarding money unnecessarily in a dream cautions against an uncharitable and darkened heart.

THE ILLUSION OF RICHES

Wealth is mankind's greatest delusion. While many believe that money holds the key to happiness – like King Midas whose dream of everything he touched turning to gold ended in despair – spending our lives in the fruitless pursuit of making money will ultimately only end in disappointment. Very few of us will ever achieve the riches we seek, while those who do will only want more, convincing themselves that they never quite have enough – until death *(right)* robs them of everything they own.

Dreaming of winning the lottery or suddenly acquiring vast wealth may seem fortuitous, but is usually interpreted as an ill omen. Dreams of winning money generally denote loss whilst, paradoxically, to dream of giving away large sums signify that the dreamer will enjoy a secure financial future.

Dreams of money set aside for a rainy day – a golden nest egg *(below)* – heralds the arrival of an unexpected piece of good news, or the sudden recovery from illness. Connected to this theme are dreams of going from rags to riches, with or without the help of others. Such visions do not usually

Dreams of THE WORLD OF WORK

Left: *'To die rich is to die in disgrace' – the skeleton taking money from the miser is Death, and shows that while we may hoard money in life it is of no possible use to us when we die.*

presage the acquisition of wealth, but signify anything of real value – energy, health in old age and self-esteem.

Visions of living the high life, jetting around the globe, sunbathing on private yachts, and shopping in London, Paris and New York may represent wish fulfilment for many, but to see these visions recurring in sleep is usually a rejoinder from the psyche to set our priorities in order – to realize that 'we are who we are' and live to our own potential, not bask in the vacuous glory of others.

Images we often associate with the rich and famous seldom hold positive connotations in dreamlore. Large stately homes and mansions may give the impression of grandeur, but hold omens that imply unforeseen misfortune in the midst of idyllic contentment. Travelling in a stretched limousine suggests a rebellious spirit that finds delight in a deliberate fondness for the 'camp and kitsch'. Fine suits and fancy dresses speak of insincere flattery and falsehood; whilst the overworked metaphor of the 'fat-cat' cigar *(left)* is emblematic of fleeting success, and the dire health risks that smoking portends.

VIOLENCE, CONFLICT AND RETRIBUTION

D reams of violence can leave us feeling shocked, especially if we are the victims of the crime – or even the perpetrator! However ghastly the images foreseen, they should not be considered a manifestation of a disturbed mind. Violence in our dreams is a way for the subconscious to unburden the anger and frustration we build up in waking life. Rather than being seen as an expression of sadistic intent, it is merely a means of unburdening emotions.

Images of war or conflict encapsulate the masculine side of the psyche. They often inform us in graphically detailed symbolism that we have an important decision to reach, or there are conflicting emotions battling away inside us. However, brutal imagery rarely portends well if the dreamer takes pleasure from the violence.

Society instills in us the idea that for all crime there must be some form of punishment, and dreams of retribution usually signify deep secrets or misdeeds that the sleeper feels they should be punished for.

Dreams of VIOLENCE, CONFLICT AND RETRIBUTION

INNER WARS

Dreaming of any form of conflict represents a battle of emotions raging within ourselves. This may be a struggle between the sleeper's desires and their conscience, or between honouring the spirit by denying the flesh. The important thing to remember is that both represent elements within ourselves, and there can be no clear right or wrong decision. Even if you make a choice that later seems to be incorrect, it is you who have made the mistake and you that has the power within you to rectify it.

Dreaming of winning a battle demonstrates that your mind has reached a decision about a problem that has been troubling you – when awake you should feel more focused and ready to tackle the predicament. However, to imagine that you lose a battle or are wounded is a warning that you need to be

cautious about how to properly solve your problems before implementing a 'solution' that may rebound on you.

To dream of joining the forces denotes that the sleeper desires a modicum of order in their life. It may be that they are finding it hard to cope with prioritizing the pressures they are currently under and would benefit from a more regimented lifestyle that, for example, the army *(above)* might offer. This should not be taken as a 'recruiting call' but merely the need to evaluate your present lifestyle.

Seeing yourself fighting in a war may be an outlet for the aggressive feelings you have suppressed in waking life, or an expression of an internal desire to prove yourself. Not all dreams of war have positive aspects, though.

*To dream of being either an ancient warrior **(right)**, a soldier on parade **(left)** or a modern soldier **(far left)** represents the same desire for glory. While they often simply reflect the dreamer's desire to be courageous, dreams of achieving glory can portend promotion at work or an advancement of status.*

CHOOSE YOUR WEAPON

Weapons represent unaddressed frustration and aggression. Freud linked this to belligerent notions of the dreamer's sexuality. Despite this somewhat simplistic view, a veritable arsenal of weapons have entered the symbolic language of the dreamscape.

The sword may be chosen by the sleeper's psyche, and if the dreamer sees themselves striking another with it, they may be lashing out in response to a perceived attack on themself. This act of aggressive self-defence is often inspired by feelings that the world is against them, although it also serves as a timely reminder that the dreamer needs to curb aggression before they inflict physical or psychological injury.

A dagger in dreams often indicates vulnerability. To find yourself attacked by someone wielding a dagger suggests that the sleeper feels scared or alone in their daily life; while to wrestle a dagger from an assailant is a sign that you will overcome your misfortunes. Arrows are associated with the Greek nymph Eros,

Below: A whole arsenal of gruesome and barbaric weaponry is available to be imagined by the sleeping mind.

the 'bringer of love' – though their appearance in dreams foreshadows times of emotional difficulty. Those who harbour secrets from their partner may find them revealed, while arguments that have boiled away beneath the surface may well erupt. However, the dreamer can restore harmony through reassurance and sincere acts of love.

Guns foretell 'trouble today, and trouble tomorrow', and are unwelcome in the dreamscape. To imagine yourself playing with a gun cautions against situations involving brinksmanship, or bluffs that might eventually have to be 'called'. To a certain extent guns mirror the phallus and thus handling a weapon in your dreams serves to emphasize the base link between violent aggression and sexuality. To see yourself shooting someone also echoes this theme of violent

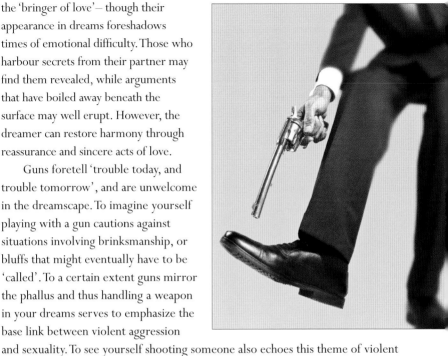

penetration. To imagine shooting yourself in the foot *(above)* is a literal warning not to bring trouble down upon yourself through foolhardy actions – you are responsible for your problems, and you alone will pay for your foolish ways!

Left: *In contrast to the symbolism of weapons, dreams involving shields offer protection and security. The dreamer may be facing problems in their waking life, but visualizing a shield promises them the strength of character to cope with whatever troubles come their way.*

OUR OWN DARK ANGELS

I n our waking lives we may suppress those feelings we know are unhealthy and destructive, yet we have little control over them in our dreams. Here emotions such as anger, envy, lust and rage – 'our own dark angels' *(right)* have more freedom to express themselves. On occasion we may even dream of performing acts that disgust and distress us – though such dreams should not necessarily be seen as negative. Such extreme expressions of our emotions can in fact exorcize these negative feelings in a way that doesn't cause harm to others and leaves us better equipped to deal with our waking lives.

Dreams in which we feel angry, or even express this anger towards others, imply that we feel stifled or belittled in daily life and are now releasing this suppressed emotion in our sleep. Similarly, feelings of rage that simmer beneath the surface may explode in acts of violent passion in our dreams. These are usually aimed against the people we blame for these feelings – people we may secretly hold grudges against, or those that have psychologically scared us in the past. Occasionally we may even attack those we love in a dream – even if they are completely blameless of any hurt – simply because they are an easy target for our aggression. While these dreams are a natural vent for internal tensions, if they become frequent and recurring, it is important that the dreamer tries to resolve exactly what is causing these inner tensions, and to calm their mind before sleep.

To imagine that you kill someone is the most extreme form of violent outpouring. For many this is simply a case of releasing the latent anger that they may hold towards that person, but for others it is a demonstration of the sleeper's jealousy toward the 'victim'. By killing them they are symbolically trying to absorb those qualities that they secretly admire.

234

UNJUST ENDS

While dreams of justice may hold a power over our conscious minds, it is the images of injustice or extreme forms of retribution that so often haunt our subconscious nightmares to reveal our guilty secrets and innermost fears.

Dreams of being judged or standing trial often make the sleeper feel uncomfortable, denoting a natural dislike of being reproached or criticized. While the dreamer rarely knows what they are standing trial for, they are almost inevitably found guilty and punished. This is the psyche's way of reproaching the dreamer for some guilty indiscretion or misdemeanour.

Dreaming of being thrown into a dark dungeon or deep pit denotes a fear of being left alone. The dreamer may feel isolated from the rest of the world, or harbour a secret that they fear, if revealed, would have devastating repercussions. To dream of being ill treated (often at the hands of a sadistic gaoler) suggests you are worried that others conspire against you, or friends will abandon and betray you.

Unless uncomfortable images and thoughts are confronted, they may fester and magnify.

To dream of being led to execution *(opposite page, centre)* implies that unless your current behaviour is curbed you run the risk of social exclusion – quite literally being 'hung out to dry'. To envision a gallows *(left)*, being burnt at the stake *(below)*, or any other form of capital punishment in a dream is a warning against pursuing a course of action you know to be wrong – the gallows acts as an ominous warning that if you persist the consequences will prove dire.

CAPTIVITY AND ESCAPE

While it is traditionally held that images of capture suggest the dreamer feels trapped within the tedium of their everyday life – and visions of escape denote an increased sense of freedom – dreams of imprisonment are much more emotive than such generalizations may suggest.

Throughout the ages, the symbolism of incarceration has shifted ground. Once thought to caution against treachery, in the late seventeenth century it developed further connotations – warning against associating with ruffians and criminals. Under Victorian morality, its omens again slipped anchor to represent the feelings of being trapped in an unhappy marriage. Finally, today it is generally accepted that dreams of captivity denote feelings of entrapment at work or in a personal relationship.

Images connected to imprisonment and restraint are represented in dreamlore. Chains *(below)* symbolize the limitations placed upon us in our everyday lives that may prevent us from achieving our goals. If the sleeper

sees themself placing a loved one in chains it is a sign that they are stifling them, or that their feelings of mistrust and jealousy are destroying the relationship. To see yourself breaking free from chains is taken as encouragement to use your own ability to better use – through strength of character your prospects will be improved.

Dreaming of being placed in jail is seldom considered auspicious, and can be an indication of the restraints the dreamer is placing upon themselves. Cell doors left open that fail to encourage escape foretell that the sleeper has little or no confidence in their own abilities and needs more self belief.

To successfully escape from incarceration foretells that the dreamer has grasped the opportunity to express themselves in a way befitting changed circumstances. However, attempting to escape but failing is a sign that there

are certain elements of the dreamer's life they need to deal with. To be seen to tunnel your way to freedom may recall feelings of claustrophobia, but offers the encouragement of success within a chosen area through perseverance.

Left: Dungeons forbode struggles in life. Though to imagine escaping from their dark depths suggests that you will come through times of trouble a stronger person.
Below:*While keys hold sexual connotations, in dreams involving incarceration they are talismanic of knowledge; by using superior intellect, you can overcome those who would hold you back, both physically and spiritually.*

A POSITIVE APPROACH TO DREAMING

M any people believe that they have no control over their dreams, but this certainly need not be the case. As already observed, our dreams can tell us a great deal about our emotions, thoughts and feelings. Keeping a dream diary is a good way of recording these, and by observing patterns and recurring themes, the sleeper can ensure that they recognize possible problems that may need attention – helping them eventually to improve both their waking and sleeping lives.

Nightmares are often deliberately pushed from our minds when we are awake as we eagerly seek to rid ourselves of disturbing images that intrude into 'real life' – they should, however, be examined with the same detail that we reserve for our more pleasant dreams. Such horrific visions invariably contain deeper truths about ourselves that we may subconsciously avoid in waking hours.

While it is unlikely that we can dictate the content of our dreams, we can at least ensure a peaceful night's sleep. By following a series of set guidelines (outlined later in this section), we can create an ambience in the bedroom that increases the likelihood of restful sleep.

REMEMBERING YOUR DREAMS AND KEEPING A DREAM DIARY

Everyone dreams. There are sleepers who, upon waking, recall their dreams better than others, yet those who only remember small snippets should not feel themselves at a disadvantage, as any recall of detail will hold significance. Keeping a dream diary can be a useful tool to interpreting your dreams and it is useful to keep a pad and pencil beside your bed so you can record your dreams when first you awake; the longer you leave the content unrecorded, the greater are the chances it will slip from your memory.

It is the emotions that lie behind our dreams that are as important as the actual images we envision. These can be expressed in a succession of vistas, or simply in one resounding image – in either case, it is important to record as much information as you can remember. Even seemingly trivial nuances that remain after our dreams have appeared to end may be significant in a final interpretation of a particular dream scenario.

Illustrated below is a list of subjects you may wish to include in your dream diary, although it is not essential always to fill in each entry, the more information you include the easier your dream will be to interpret. This list should not be considered conclusive and can be adapted by the dreamer

Right: *By noting as much information about your dream as possible you should be able to understand your dreams better. However, even if you can't fill in all the suggested responses, it can still prove a useful exercise and aide-memoire to refer back to at a later date.*

DREAM DIARY

Date of dream:

Day of the week:

People involved in the dream:

Mood and feelings expressed:

Prominent colours:

What story did the dream enact?:

Problems and conflicts encountered:

How were problems

Did the dream occur

Prominent symbols:

Repeated elements

How did the dream

Conclusions:

n?:

ast or present?:

t dreams:

to suit their individual need. For example, some people find it beneficial to grade their dream on a scale of 1 to 10 – where 1 represents a terrifying nightmare, and 10 signifies a wonderfully uplifting and spiritual dream. Others may like to add a box explaining how they felt before their dream and how they feel afterwards. However it is adapted, a dream diary can grant the dreamer a significant insight into their emotional wellbeing and help them understand the nature of their dreams.

243

BANISHING NIGHTMARES

Nightmares are the most misunderstood of all dreams. They are too often dismissed as representing nothing more than the distressed images of an over-imaginative mind. Unlike sweeter dreams, we rarely try to recall the images that have so troubled us. To do so stirs up many frightful thoughts; however, if we stop and re-enter our nightmare it will reveal important, deeper truths that often fail to surface in tranquil dreams.

In the past it was believed that nightmares were caused by demons – known as 'incubus' – who preyed especially on women and the young. In fact, in some societies nightmares were considered a symbol of a weak or undisciplined mind. Another explanation was that they were caused by the malicious thoughts of others, and to experience a nightmare was a sign that someone was wishing you ill or even that they planned to harm. Because of this people would try to protect themselves from bad dreams in a variety of different ways, ranging from hiding amulets, especially a crucifix, under their pillow, to reciting incantations and prayers.

Modern dream analysts agree that, although they can seem distressing at the time, nightmares are in fact a healthy expression of deep-seated fears

Left: The artist Hieronymus Bosch imagined a nightmarish world of grotesque monsters who extracted vengeance for past sin. Today, echoes of these disquieting characters may still lurk at the dark margins of our dreamscape.

Right: Images of hell are common in nightmares because they represent the fear of retribution. However, as with all bad dreams it is important to remember that, as frightening as they seem, they are designed for our personal benefit and can do no physical harm.

and tensions. Such images represent the dreamer's desire to deal with their problems rather than simply hiding from them. By arousing feelings of pent-up tension, these emotions are released in our sleep and we are able to unburden them.

However shocking a nightmare might appear, it is important to remember that they are not omens of evil – in fact, such dreams prevent bad fortune by liberating us from negative feelings, making us more likely to act upon reasoned judgement than suppressed emotion.

In our daily lives we are bombarded with images of suffering and violence. We see them on the news, in films and on television programmes. Thus our minds absorb a huge amount of negative imagery – which, when combined with feelings of suppression, guilt or frustration, reappear in our dreamscape.

Nightmares scare us because they contain graphic images we would rather not imagine, and so we often dismiss them immediately. However, if we were to look deeper into these dreams, we would discover important messages. This is especially true if we see ourselves tackling our worst fears because we all have the ability (if not the will power) to overcome our phobias.

Often a nightmare will jolt you awake, sweating and in a dishevelled state: regain your composure, then try to re-enter the dream, but this time forearmed with the confident knowledge that whatever the worst of your personal

Left: Images of monsters such as the hideous Medusa can be deeply distressing, though to overcome your enemy is an extremely positive sign which foretells of good fortune and inner strength.

demons can do to you, they always lack the ability to harm you. Once they are seen for the impostors they truly are, you can begin to fight back. By far the most effective way of doing this is to use humour against your tormentors. For example, if your sleep is plagued by the vision of a vampire, take away his cloak and imagine a pink polka dot skirt in its place... what possible harm can he do to you now?

Another effective method for removing menace from nightmares (which works particularly well for children), is to draw the fears that haunt you in sleep on a sheet of paper, then add a bright sun in the sky, and turn the dour black of your worst fears into a multitude of vibrant colours; by adding jollity and humour to your imaginative armoury, you create a strong weapon which becomes available for you to use whenever nightmares threaten.

SWEET DREAMS

Sweet dreams require an untroubled and relaxing sleep in order for the body to awaken properly rested and reinvigorated. Here are my ten personal tips for achieving a good night's sleep.

1 Try not to worry about the amount of sleep you are having. The quantity of sleep we need each night varies considerably. Often we either overestimate the time we need to have actually slept, or underestimate the total amount we have had. Even on a seemingly sleepless night, we actually sleep for a lot longer than we may think.

2 Live an active life. If you have trouble falling asleep at night it may be that your body is not tired. Exercise encourages the body to seek rest and will result in a deeper and more rewarding sleep. If you tend to nap during the day, this may interfere with your sleeping pattern.

3 Make sure you are fully relaxed. Before going to bed lessen your tension with a massage, do some light exercise or go for a gentle walk. A warm bath (not too hot!) may also help you to unwind, though a shower is more likely to rouse you rather than help you sleep.

4 Don't go to bed on a full stomach. Leave at least two hours between your last meal and when you go to bed. Digestion can affect your sleeping pattern and may result in strange dreams (this is true whatever you eat and is not restricted to just cheese!). If you insist on eating before sleep, ensure it is something light such as a piece of fruit rather than a full meal.

5 Avoid stimulating your body. Caffeine drinks such as tea or coffee will prolong the time it takes for you to fall asleep, whilst alcohol and tobacco will inhibit rapid eye movement (REM) and prolong the period of light sleep when you are most likely to be disturbed by external influences. For those who wish to drink before going to sleep, water or warm milk is advisable.

6 Make sure your bed is comfortable. We spend almost a third of our lives in bed, so it is important that we ensure that it is as comfortable as possible.

Ideally the mattress should be firm but not hard, while the spine should be kept at the same contour as when you are standing upright. This will provide optimum support for your body, a comfortable position for your arms and legs, and ensure you achieve peaceful rest.

7 Ensure the bedroom conditions are comfortable. Your bedroom should be neither too hot, nor too cold (a temperature between 16–18 °C/60–65 °F, is generally considered comfortable). The room should be dark (light is our bodies' natural cue to wake) and all external noise should be as muffled as possible. Playing recordings from nature, for example the sound of waterfalls and waves, is an effective way of drowning out other noises; these natural sounds also recall the pulse-like noises we subconsciously remember from within our mother's womb, relaxing us further.

8 Keep a notebook by your bed to record any thoughts that are worrying you. The stresses and strains of our daily lives continue to trouble us while we are trying to fall asleep. There is little we can do about them late at night or early in the morning, but keeping a note pad by the bed allows us to jot down our thoughts and stops us from pondering them and allowing them to disturb our sleep. Once you have written your thoughts down, they will keep until the morning… they require no further consideration when you are trying to sleep.

9 Go to bed 30 minutes before going to sleep. It is important to relax your mind before going to sleep. Reading a book can help clear your mind of the troubles of the day, although try to ensure that it is not too taxing on your concentration or too absorbing, or your brain will concentrate too heavily on the book and is less likely to relax your mind.

10 Relax. If you feel as though you can't sleep or you wake in the middle of the night, try not to worry about it. Worry will just activate your mind and ensure that you find it harder to drift off. Consign persistent, intrusive worries to the notepad mentioned in Tip 8. If you find that you still can't relax your mind, read for a while, or try to think of a place or person that makes you feel safe and secure. By focusing on an image that comforts you, your mind will relax again and you will find it easier to slip off to sleep.

The following simple relaxation technique may help you if you are still having trouble sleeping.

Make yourself comfortable in bed and imagine your body sinking into your mattress. Tense your toes and hold them tightly tensed for a slow count of five, then release them and concentrate on how relaxed they feel. Repeat this process for all the major muscle groups in your body, working your way up from the calves in your lower legs to the thighs, buttocks and stomach, then from your chest all the way down your arms to your fingers, and finally on to your shoulders, neck and head. At the release of each tension, concentrate hard on how relaxed you feel in the respective parts of the body and allow yourself to drift off to sleep.

INDEX

ACKNOWLEDGEMENTS

The authors and publishers would like to thank the following
for their kind permission to reproduce their photographs:
Jack Clucas: 46(in), 47(br), 68(tl), 78, 79(br), 81(br),
85(all 5 images), 86(tr), 86(br) and 87(br).
John Paul Cook: 79(br), 92(tr), 93(t), 93(b), 105 and 176(b).
Patrick Hook: 94(b), 96 and 102(bl).
Author's own photographs: 17, 23(i), 27(br), 28, 29(t), 36, 42(tl),
42(b), 67(bg), 77(in), 79(tr), 79(bl), 81(t), 83(tl), 87(tr), 101(br),
132(b), 133(br), 165(i), 166, 167(t), 169, 174(b), 175(t) and 179.
Thomas Schoch page 15 www.retas.de/thomas
Thanks also to Hazel Clucas for permission to show her
jewellery design on page 65 www.hazelclucas.co.uk